IN

There are many medi[...]ons of
tales told by different n[...]aucer
was no doubt familiar with some of these—in particular with
the *Decameron* and the *Filocolo* of Boccaccio, one of his favourite
authors. But *The Canterbury Tales* is the only such collection in
which the tellers do not belong to a single social class, but form
a cross-section of different social and human types. The great
advantage of this invention of Chaucer's was that it made possible
a dramatic relationship between the pilgrims and the stories they
tell: we are able to see a particular tale as expressing the personality of its teller, and this will allow us not only to understand
the personality more fully, but also to see the tale itself in a new
light—sometimes the wavering light of irony. This dramatic
potential in the whole scheme of *The Canterbury Tales* was
recognized long ago. In 1912 the American scholar G. L. Kittredge wrote: 'Structurally regarded, *The Canterbury Tales* is a
kind of Human Comedy. From this point of view, the Pilgrims
are the *dramatis personae*, and their stories are only speeches that
are somewhat longer than common, entertaining in and for themselves (to be sure), but primarily significant, in each case, because
they illustrate the speaker's character and opinions, or show the
relations of the travelers to one another in the progressive action
of the Pilgrimage.'[1] We can see now that in the excitement of
his insight into the *Tales* Kittredge somewhat exaggerated his
case. With some of the tales, certainly, there is the closest possible relationship between story and teller; this is true of the
Pardoner, the Merchant, or the Canon's Yeoman. But in other
cases, such as those of the Knight or the Cook, there is only a
general appropriateness in the tale told (often an appropriateness
based on social class), while in still others, such as the Man of
Law's or the Physician's, there seems to be no particular reason
why tale and teller should be linked, or at least we can learn

[1] 'Chaucer's Discussion of Marriage', *Modern Philology*, IX
(1911–12). The whole essay is of great interest for its discussion of *The
Franklin's Tale*. It is more easily available as reprinted in *Chaucer:
Modern Essays in Criticism*, ed. E. Wagenknecht (Oxford University
Press, 1959).

nothing from the connexion. In the case of the Franklin, there is not that burning urgency of self-expression that we find with the Pardoner or the Merchant, fusing the tale and all its surrounding material into an irresistible dramatic monologue. But *The Franklin's Tale* is certainly very carefully chosen to fit the Franklin, and the link between them is of an unusually subtle, paradoxical, and even problematic kind. Each sets the other in a new perspective; each mirrors the other, so that we have reflexions within reflexions in an almost unending series. For this reason, the present Introduction will begin with a close scrutiny of the description of the Franklin in *The General Prologue* and, more particularly, of *The Franklin's Prologue* which immediately precedes the Tale itself. Both of these passages are included in the present edition, the former as an appendix and the latter as part of the Tale.

THE PORTRAIT OF THE FRANKLIN

James Winny remarks, in his edition of *The General Prologue* in this series, that in the description of the Franklin 'Chaucer returns to the infectious gaiety of mood in which he describes the Squire'. He is elderly yet in good health, a combination beautifully caught in the single line

> Whit was his berd as is the dayesie,

which at once describes his beard's colour, thereby indicating his advanced years, and suggests natural vigour and freshness. The Franklin is a man of substance and importance. There has been some discussion as to what the word *franklin* (or, in line 362 of *The General Prologue*, *vavasour*) implied about a man's social status. It means literally a freeholder, one who possesses land absolutely, not temporarily or in return for dues or services. By the fourteenth century it seems to have come to be the name of a class of landowners below the class of the nobility and yet roughly the equivalents of gentlemen. In some circumstances perhaps a franklin would be thought the social equal of a knight or an esquire, but this Franklin, evidently a rich country squire, is clearly outside the magic circle of chivalry represented by the Knight and his son. It is equally clear, as we shall see, that he aspires to be inside it. In his own *contree* he is absolute master, just as the Prioress is mistress in her convent, but, like her,

THE FRANKLIN'S PROLOGUE AND TALE

FROM THE CANTERBURY TALES

BY

GEOFFREY CHAUCER

Edited with Introduction, Notes and Glossary by

A. C. SPEARING

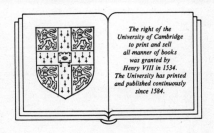

The right of the
University of Cambridge
to print and sell
all manner of books
was granted by
Henry VIII in 1534.
The University has printed
and published continuously
since 1584.

CAMBRIDGE UNIVERSITY PRESS

CAMBRIDGE
NEW YORK   PORT CHESTER
MELBOURNE   SYDNEY

Published by the Press Syndicate of the University of Cambridge
The Pitt Building, Trumpington Street, Cambridge CB2 1RP
40 West 20th Street, New York, NY 10011–4211, USA
10 Stamford Road, Oakleigh, Melbourne 3166, Australia

Library of Congress catalogue card number: 66–16666

ISBN 0 521 04624 6

First published 1966
Reprinted 1971
Reprinted with corrections 1972
Seventeenth printing 1991

Printed in Great Britain at the
University Press, Cambridge

CONTENTS

ACKNOWLEDGEMENTS

This edition owes much to the only previous separate edition of *The Franklin's Tale* to be published in England, that of Professor Phyllis Hodgson (Athlone Press, 1960). Though I often disagree with Professor Hodgson's critical assessments, I have found her work a mine of valuable information, particularly on medieval astrology and astronomy.

In addition to works mentioned in notes and footnotes, I am also much indebted to James Sledd, 'Dorigen's Complaint', *Modern Philology*, XLV (1947–8)—surely the finest piece of criticism on *The Franklin's Tale* yet published—and to the following: R. Blenner-Hassett, 'Autobiographical Aspects of Chaucer's Franklin', *Speculum*, XXVIII (1953); Germaine Dempster, 'Chaucer at Work on the Complaint in *The Franklin's Tale*', *Modern Language Notes*, LII (1937); G. H. Gerould, 'The Social Status of Chaucer's Franklin', *Publications of the Modern Language Association of America*, XLI (1926); J. S. P. Tatlock, *The Scene of The Franklin's Tale Visited* (London, 1914).

In various places I refer readers requiring further information or comment to *An Introduction to Chaucer*, by the three editors of this series of texts.

A. C. S.

Cambridge
September 1965

when he is brought into contact with the chivalric and the courtly, he feels a certain unease, which expresses itself partly in assertiveness and partly in excessive humility. In *The General Prologue*, however, we see him in his own world, and very much in command of it. He is rich and enjoys his wealth. He loves good food and drink, and loves sharing his plenty with others: he is the Saint Julian, the patron saint of hospitality, in his part of the world. But he is not a man with whom his servants can afford to take liberties or fall below strict standards of service:

> Wo was his cook but if his sauce were
> Poynaunt and sharp, and redy al his geere.

He has held important offices, having been president of the magistrates' court, 'knight of the shire' or member of Parliament, and sheriff and county auditor. These offices are a sign not merely of his importance but of his possessing a substantial amount of legal knowledge. It is no doubt for this reason that he is described in *The General Prologue* as riding along in the company of the Man of Law.

So far as it is explicit, this portrait of the Franklin seems to be largely favourable. The question of social status, which it is necessary to mention here in order to explain what a franklin is, is not raised in *The General Prologue*, and we are left with an impression of vigour and confidence. But, as Mr Winny goes on to write, 'it is hard to believe that Chaucer's critical discernment is entirely suspended, or that the man who shows such respect for the self-abnegating spirit of the Knight and the Parson regards the Franklin's epicurean life with complete approval'. The principle by which his life is lived is stated clearly by Chaucer:

> To liven in delit was evere his wone,
> For he was Epicurus owene sone,
> That heeld opinioun that pleyn delit
> Was verray felicitee parfit.

Superficially, these words seem to offer plain statement, with no indication of approval or disapproval. But the very language used supplies a higher standard by which the Franklin's principle of conduct is to be judged. *Felicitee* is most commonly used not simply of happiness but of the true happiness of heaven. Once we respond to this connotation of the word, we recognize that Epicurus and the Franklin are mistaken in their assessment of

3

where true happiness lies. In finding happiness in *pleyn delit*, sensual pleasure, the Franklin is a flawed creature, and we shall be prepared to find flaws elsewhere in his values.[1]

Most of the characteristics touched on in *The General Prologue* portrait are reflected in one way or another in *The Franklin's Tale*, though not necessarily in the most obvious way. It is the richness and variety of food in his house that is most stressed in *The General Prologue*, but this is not the main subject of his story, for it is not where his aspirations lie. His heart may be in his belly, but it aspires to higher things. His Tale is concerned with *gentillesse* and *franchise*, aristocratic virtues with a spiritual grace about them, but his love of good living creeps into small local details. Thus the magician in his Tale keeps up a standard of hospitality that reminds us of the Franklin's own house-keeping—

> Hem lakked no vitaille that mighte hem plese.
> So wel arrayed hous as ther was oon
> Aurelius in his lyf saugh nevere noon   (514–16)

—and his attitude towards his servants in matters connected with food is also reminiscent of the Franklin's:

> To him this maister called his squier,
> And seyde him thus: 'Is redy oure soper?
> Almoost an houre it is, I undertake,
> Sith I yow bad oure soper for to make'.   (537–40)

Aurelius evidently entertains the Clerk on a comparable scale, for when the Clerk refuses to take any money for his services his excuse is that 'Thou hast ypayed wel for my vitaille' (947). Clearly *vitaille* is no trivial matter in the minds of the Franklin's characters. Moreover, when he chooses an elaborate rhetorical periphrasis to state the time of year when the Clerk carries out his experiment, giving a verbal equivalent for an illumination in a medieval Calendar, the scene he describes includes Janus as an English franklin, enjoying seasonable food and drink:

> Janus sit by the fyr, with double berd,
> And drinketh of his bugle horn the wyn;
> Biforn him stant brawen of the tusked swyn,
> And 'Nowel' crieth every lusty man.   (580–3)

[1] In *The Merchant's Tale* (ed. Hussey, ll. 809–10) we are told that 'Summe clerkes holden that felicitee Stant in delit', and the context makes it clear that it is foolish to live on this assumption.

4

This is surely the Franklin himself, of whom we have been told in *The General Prologue* that

> After the sondry sesons of the yeer,
> So chaunged he his mete and his soper.

A second characteristic from *The General Prologue* portrait of the Franklin that is reflected in his Tale is his knowledge of and interest in the law. This, however, is a far more central theme in the Tale, and will best be considered later.

'THE FRANKLIN'S PROLOGUE'

Nothing more is heard of the Franklin after *The General Prologue* until we come to the Prologue to his own Tale. Although *The Franklin's Prologue* (in which I include the link-passage headed in some manuscripts 'Heere folwen the wordes of the Frankeleyn to the Squier, and the wordes of the Hoost to the Frankeleyn') is comparatively short, it will repay careful study. It is seemingly casual and even gossipy, with the Franklin digressing as an old man might to shake his head over his son's evil ways and being sharply called to order by the Host, but it is in fact extremely subtle. In it a number of the most important themes of the Tale itself are raised, and the Prologue is used as a means of directing our attitudes towards those themes and towards the Franklin. It is a perfect example of Chaucer's mature art, unpressed, urbane, with none of the packed quality of a Donne or a Hopkins, and yet with every word counting.

'THE SQUIRE'S TALE' AND THE FRANKLIN'S INTERRUPTION

The Franklin's Prologue follows on from *The Squire's Tale*. The Squire is the son of the Knight: a young aristocrat, accomplished as a warrior and courtier, dressed in the height of fashion, and full of enthusiasm and *joie de vivre*. He is, like his father, a typical figure rather than an individual like the Wife of Bath or the Pardoner—he could appear in a medieval allegory as Youth. He tells a tale that is entirely in keeping with this typical character: a chivalric romance, exotic in its setting and full of improbable wonders in its action, and yet concerning characters who are models of aristocratic behaviour. The Squire's attitude towards his marvellous story is one of naïf enthusiasm: all the characters are perfect of their kind, and wonders are heaped breathlessly on wonders—a horse of brass that will carry its rider wherever he chooses within a day, a mirror that will disclose friends and enemies and true and false lovers, a ring that will enable one to understand the language of the birds, a sword that will pierce any armour but will also heal the wound, a hawk that has had an unhappy love-affair. The Squire moves from one wonder to the next, himself as astonished and delighted as he would wish his listeners to be, and gradually becoming more and more thoroughly lost in the complications of his narrative. He ends Part II of his Tale with a desperate attempt to pull the different threads of the narrative together and an enthusiastic promise of more *mervailles* and complications to follow:

> Thus lete I Canacee hir hauk keping;
> I wol namoore as now speke of hir ring,
> Til it come eft to purpos for to seyn
> How that this faucon gat hire love ageyn
> Repentant, as the storie telleth us,
> By mediacion of Cambalus,
> The kinges sone, of which that I yow tolde,
> But hennesforth I wol my proces holde
> To speken of aventures and of batailles,
> That nevere yet was herd so grete mervailles!
> First wol I telle yow...
> And after wol I speke...
> And after wol I speke...
> And ther I lefte I wol ageyn biginne.

He begins on Part III, but after only two lines, before he has completed his first sentence, the Franklin interrupts him, and *The Squire's Tale* is, as Milton put it, 'left half told'. Let us look more closely at the words in which the Franklin interrupts him:

> 'In feith, Squier, thow hast thee wel yquit
> And gentilly. I preise wel thy wit,'
> Quod the Frankeleyn, 'consideringe thy yowthe,
> So feelingly thou spekest, sire, I allow the.
> As to my doom, ther is noon that is heere
> Of eloquence that shal be thy peere,
> If that thou live; God yeve thee good chaunce,
> And in vertu sende thee continuaunce!
> For of thy speche I have greet deyntee.'   (1–9)

Introduction

One thing to be said about this little speech is that it is a masterpiece of tact. It contains nothing but praise of the Squire and his Tale, but it is absolutely final in bringing him to a stop before he can get entangled in any more *grete mervailles*. No television interviewer could be more skilful in bringing a garrulous member of the public politely to a halt. The very length of the Franklin's praise creates an interruption long enough to make it impossible for the Squire to resume his unfinished sentence, and the last line is magnificently and confidently dismissive—the Franklin is pleased, the final verdict has been given, and there is no more to be said on that subject. There is tact and tact, however, and the difference between kinds of tact will emerge from a comparison. At another point in *The Canterbury Tales* (later than this according to some manuscripts and earlier according to others), another pilgrim, the Monk, is interrupted before he has finished his Tale. He has been telling a long and doleful series of tragic short stories, he has gone on for too long, and the Knight interrupts him. He does so, not by praising him at length, but by saying that his subject-matter is too distressing:

> ...for litel hevinesse
> Is right ynough to muche folk, I gesse.
> I seye for me, it is a greet disese,
> Whereas men han been in greet welthe and ese,
> To heeren of hire sodeyn fal, allas!

This interruption is less fulsome in praise than the Franklin's, but it is also less assuming. It implies that the Monk's stories have worked, in making people feel unhappy, it offers no general verdict on his achievement, and it leaves the Monk free to continue with stories of a less depressing kind if he wishes. In a word, the Knight, though he is unquestionably the man of highest social rank among the pilgrims, does not raise himself to a position of superiority over the person he interrupts; the Franklin does. The Knight displays true good breeding (or, as we might say, *gentillesse*), while the Franklin's tact is accompanied by a good deal of patronage. There is a world of presumption in his 'consideringe thy yowthe', with the deliberating pause before it imposed by the inserted 'Quod the Frankeleyn'. This patronizing attitude is continued in 'If that thou live', which defers the Squire's achievement in eloquence to a distant future, and even hints at the threat that that future may not, after all, arrive.

7

Introduction

We seem to see, in the Franklin's opening lines, the tact of a man who is determined to assert and maintain his own social standing.

Gentillesse

One way in which he does this is by showing that he can recognize the aristocratic virtues in others. It is noticeable that in his first sentence he praises the Squire for having acquitted himself as a story-teller *gentilly*. *Gentillesse* is going to be a key concept in *The Franklin's Tale*, and the Franklin himself forces us to say something about it at this early stage. It is a word which has no exact equivalent in modern English, because it draws its meaning from a scale of values—a conception of society and of human nature—which has ceased to exist. Medieval society was rigidly divided on a class basis, and this division leads to a conception of the virtues and vices which is, as we should say, neither purely ethical nor purely social, but a mixture of the two. Thus *gentil* is a word which can mean simply aristocratic, as it probably does when we are told of the pilgrims' reaction to *The Knight's Tale* that they all admired it, 'And namely the gentils everichon'— and especially each of the *gentil* people. But *gentil* normally also implies not mere social status but a particular standard of behaviour, which may include anything from the social graces to moral virtue itself. Of course medieval people knew as well as we do that those of noble birth do not always behave nobly (this indeed is an argument put forward at some length in *The Wife of Bath's Tale*), and equally that noble behaviour is not confined to the aristocracy (which is what the Franklin himself argues). But they did expect there to be some connexion between the two: they felt that high birth ought to produce generosity, magnanimity, courtesy, compassion, refinement. Similarly at the other end of the social scale: those of the lowest class were called *cherls*, but this was a word which it was hardly possible to use in a neutral sense (as we might use the word 'proletariat'), because *cherlissh* referred to the kind of behaviour they expected of such a person—coarse, mean, rude, selfish. The connexion between social standing and behaviour is made by Chaucer himself in *The Miller's Prologue*, directly after he has said that the *gentils* particularly enjoyed *The Knight's Tale*. He apologizes in advance for any indecency in *The Miller's Tale* by saying that 'The Millere is a cherl, ye knowe wel this' and therefore, as a

8

matter of course, he will tell 'a cherles tale in his manere'. Here then, Chaucer is referring behaviour of a literary kind to social class; and to a modern reader it is very striking how deeply the medieval class-system had penetrated even into ideas about literature. Both the literary *genres* and the styles that go with them were distinguished in the Middle Ages on a class basis. It is therefore natural that the Knight and the Squire should tell stories belonging to the genre of chivalric romance, whose characters were *gentil* by birth and behaved in a *gentil* manner, and which were written in the 'high style' taught by textbooks of rhetoric. There is thus a triple connexion between moral virtue, high birth, and elaborate eloquence; and this is what we find in this first passage of *The Franklin's Prologue*. The Franklin praises the aristocratic young man for having acquitted himself *gentilly*, then for his *eloquence*, and then for his *vertu*. If the modern reader finds the juxtaposition of virtue and eloquence somewhat surprising, he must remember that *gentillesse* is the link between them.

THE FRANKLIN, HIS SON, AND THE HOST

Having brought the Squire to a definite stop, the Franklin is able to relax a little, and he begins to reminisce on a subject suggested by the Squire himself. This second passage of his speech is thus closely connected with the first, and is linked to it even by rhyme. It too will be worth close attention:

> I have a sone, and by the Trinitee,
> I hadde levere than twenty pound worth lond,
> Though it right now were fallen in myn hond,.
> He were a man of swich discrecioun
> As that ye been. Fy on possessioun,
> But if a man be vertuous withal!
> I have my sone snybbed, and yet shal,
> For he to vertu listeth nat entende;
> But for to pleye at dees, and to despende
> And lese al that he hath, is his usage.
> And he hath levere talken with a page
> Than to comune with any gentil wight
> Where he mighte lerne gentillesse aright. (10–22)

Seeing the Squire, the Knight's son, makes the Franklin think of his own son, and the comparison between them is very much

9

to his son's disadvantage. The comparison, like much that the Franklin says, has an interestingly double effect. He is at the same time admitting that there is a great gap between the Squire and his son and, in making the comparison at all, putting them on the same level. He envies the Squire's *discrecioun*, *vertu* and *gentillesse* on his son's behalf, but in doing so he is implicitly claiming that his son *ought* to possess these aristocratic virtues. The image which Chaucer makes the Franklin choose to enforce the comparison is admirably selected to display his character. It would please him more to have a son comparable with the Squire than to receive land worth twenty pounds a year, even though it were to come into his possession at this very moment! Thus, in the very breath in which he is extolling the virtues of spirit appropriate to a young aristocrat, he betrays that his real interest is in material values. The great landowner measures virtue against land with no sense of incongruity. The point is rammed home in his next sentence: the very fact that he needs to assert that material possessions are of no value without *vertu* indicates that this is not the assumption on which he usually acts. We cannot imagine the Knight saying such a thing. The whole character of the Franklin is laid bare in two casual sentences, without any of that explicit confession of motive that is so common a convention in medieval literature. And this process of laying bare continues as the Franklin says more about his son. He imagines that scolding him might make him pursue *vertu*. Then it becomes clear that what really irks him in his son's dissolute behaviour is that he loses money in gambling; perhaps it would worry him less if he *won* at dice. Finally, he is dissatisfied with the company his son keeps, and *gentil* and *gentillesse* pop up again, with a telling insistence. It is easy to imagine how often they have been mentioned in the Franklin's scoldings of his son. No wonder he preferred to spend his time and his father's money in the gambling den.

Gentillesse has been mentioned too often for the Host already, and he protests with his usual bluntness. Once the Franklin has got started on this, evidently his favourite subject, there is no knowing when he will come to a stop. Fear of an extended moral disquisition, either too private or too abstract, seems to be the Host's main motive for his interruption, though no doubt he also feels that there is something odd in the constant appearance of these particular terms on the Franklin's lips. And so he reminds him of the pilgrims' agreement to tell stories on their way. The Franklin's answer shows an extraordinary deference, indeed almost an obsequiousness, towards the Host. It is as if he were answering the protest about *gentillesse* with an exaggerated parody of *gentil* behaviour, but it is difficult to tell how far the exaggeration is intended. It may be that Chaucer intends us to see the Franklin as thoroughly confused in his social behaviour: having put the Squire, who is *gentil*, firmly in his place, he is now showing extreme politeness towards a *cherl*. But this would make the Franklin into a gross caricature of a *parvenu*, and he seems really to be depicted with great subtlety. Certainly his last words to the Host, making him, of all people, the supreme arbiter of taste in literary matters, sound like an intentional irony:

> I prey to God that it may plesen yow;
> Thanne woot I wel that it is good ynow.   (35–6)

He then begins on a preface to his actual tale.

We have learned a great deal about the Franklin from these opening passages of his Prologue, though, since we have learned it obliquely and by implication, rather than by direct statement, it may be that we have misinterpreted certain details. There are five hundred years between us and Chaucer, and, however accomplished his art of implication, we are bound to lose some details of social observation through the passage of time. But it seems safe to say that the Franklin has been revealed as a man uneasy about his relationship to the chivalric world represented by the Knight and the Squire. To describe him as a *parvenu* or *nouveau riche* would be too crude: from *The General Prologue* it is clear that, in his own milieu, he is a man of established position and authority. But he aspires to more than this, and is obsessed by chivalric qualities of spirit which can be summed up under the heading of *gentillesse*. All this prepares us very exactly for the tale he is going to tell: it will take the form of a competition in *gentillesse*, and its aim will be to prove that this quality is open to those outside the charmed circle of chivalry. But, since we have been allowed to see through and into the Franklin himself, we may expect that we shall also be able to see more deeply into his Tale than he himself can, and to find in it meanings of which he is unaware.

Introduction

The Franklin begins the preface to his Tale by asserting that he has taken it from a particular original, a Breton lay, and in doing so he raises for us the whole question of the Tale's sources. We might otherwise be prepared to 'lat slepen that is stille', and leave the source problem to be studied for its own sake by those who are so inclined; but, since the Franklin himself raises it, it is clearly relevant to our understanding of the actual Tale. His statement that his source is a Breton lay is quite un-equivocal:

> Thise olde gentil Britouns in hir dayes
> Of diverse aventures maden layes,
> Rimeyed in hir firste Briton tonge;
> Whiche layes with hir instrumentz they songe,
> Or elles redden hem for hir plesaunce,
> And oon of hem have I in remembraunce,
> Which I shal seyn with good wil as I kan.   (37–43)

With this there might seem to be no arguing. But one point must be made clear from the very beginning: in medieval litera-ture, such claims to a specific source are not necessarily to be taken as literal truth. Medieval works of literature are nearly always based on a source outside themselves, and it is one of the basic assumptions of treatises on the art of poetry that the *materia* or subject-matter of a particular work will be supplied as a *donnée*, not invented by the writer himself. Surprising as it may seem to us, living after the Romantic movement has transformed older ideas about literature, in the Middle Ages authority was prized more highly than originality. Hence a writer would nearly always refer to an authoritative source for his material. But the particular source he referred to might itself be part of his fiction. In the poem *Sir Gawain and the Green Knight*, for example, written by an unknown contemporary of Chaucer, we are assured that the story has been told as it was written down 'in the best boke of romaunce', yet, despite many years of scholarly inquiry, no specific source for it has ever been found. The same thing is found elsewhere in Chaucer himself. He tells us that the story of his poem *Troilus and Criseyde* is taken from a Latin author called Lollius, yet it is clear beyond question that his real source, which he often follows in every detail, is a poem by the Italian Boccaccio, and no Lollius has ever been discovered. We must therefore approach the source problem in *The Franklin's Tale* with an open mind.

In claiming a Breton lay for the source of his Tale, the Franklin is relating it to a specific literary genre. The earliest Breton lays known are those by Marie de France, a French poet of the late twelfth century. She claims that she is simply repeating stories told by Breton minstrels, and it seems likely that she was herself the inventor of the genre as a written form. Her lays are short poems, dealing with the romantic adventures of aristocratic characters, and often involving magic or the supernatural (these last being typically Celtic elements). Her characters are essentially types, and her plots are often not fully integrated, but the lays generally have a definite, if thin, charm and elegance. From this it will be clear that *The Franklin's Tale* is not really like a Breton lay at all. It does contain a large supernatural element, but this is not left as a Celtic mystery, but is explained in detail as 'scientific' natural magic or as illusion. It does begin with aristocratic characters of an idealized and typified kind—Dorigen, for example, is 'oon the faireste under sonne'—but at the crucial points in the narrative these are developed in such a way that we come to take a keen interest in them as individuals. The narrative itself is admirably ordered. Moreover, while Marie's lays generally deal with love outside marriage, and present this as the normal form of interesting human relationship, the Franklin focuses his attention upon the relationship of the married couple Dorigen and Arveragus. The attempt of the squire Aurelius to break up this relationship by having an illicit affair with Dorigen is prevented by his own innate decency; while, if *The Franklin's Tale* were really a Breton lay, his affair with Dorigen would be the emotional and imaginative centre of the work.

The Franklin's Tale, then, though it has some superficial similarities to the Breton lays, is not really like enough to them for us to believe that it has one as its source. A further point is that there is no evidence in the Tale to suggest that Chaucer had actually read any Breton lays. A scholar who has studied the question in detail writes that 'Not only has no Breton lay source ever been found for this tale, but no Celtic analogue is known

for any considerable part of it'.[1] The only suggestion of a link
with the Breton lays is found in the information about them
supplied by lines 37–43, quoted above, and it is particularly
striking that, while this information partly overlaps with some
of that supplied in extant French lays, it corresponds much more
exactly with what can be found in a preface prefixed to two
English versions of lays. These English lays—*Lai le Freine* and
Sir Orfeo—are both found in a manuscript dating from the early
fourteenth century and probably written in London. It seems
quite possible that Chaucer knew this very manuscript, and that
all he knew about lays is derived from it. One significant detail
is that he makes the Franklin say that the lays were originally
written in the Breton language—'Rimeyed in hir firste Briton
tonge'—and, while this is not a statement made in any of the
extant French lays, it is implied by a line in the English *Lai le
Freine*.

Whether or not Chaucer actually knew any of the French lays,
it seems clear that he did not make much use of them in writing
The Franklin's Tale, and we are left free to look elsewhere for
its origin. The basic narrative material of the Tale—Dorigen's
promise to Aurelius that she would become his mistress and her
husband's consent that she should keep her promise—is to be
found in one form or another in many traditional stories. It is
sufficiently widespread to have been classified by students of
folklore under the title of 'The Damsel's Rash Promise'. As is
often the case with medieval popular stories, the oldest known
versions are not European but oriental. It is the European versions, however, which introduce a magician into the story, and,
of the various extant European versions, one in particular seems
to be closest to Chaucer's poem. This is the story which is told
twice by the fourteenth-century Italian poet Boccaccio, once as
a mere incident in the *Filocolo*, and once as a complete tale in
the *Decameron*. Even here, however, there is little detailed corre-
spondence with *The Franklin's Tale* either in words or in
incidents, though there are a few details that are found in *The
Franklin's Tale* and the *Filocolo* or the *Decameron* but not in the
other parallel stories. Among these are the fact that the magician's
art depends on the moon, the performance of his experiment in
early January, and the choice of a large sum of money to reward

[1] L. H. Loomis, 'Chaucer and the Breton Lays of the Auchinleck
MS', *Studies in Philology*, XXXVIII (1941).

him. Since Boccaccio was one of Chaucer's favourite poets, and one to whom he is greatly indebted elsewhere in his work, it seems very likely that Chaucer had read either or both of his versions of the story before writing *The Franklin's Tale*. But there is no sign that in writing the Tale he was working with a copy of either of these versions before him, as he must have written *Troilus and Criseyde*, for example, with a copy of Boccaccio's *Filostrato* before him. It seems much more likely that the position is the same as with a number of other *Canterbury Tales*: Chaucer is not, as he usually did in his earlier work, 'translating' and combining certain written sources, but is composing freely on the basis of a traditional story. It is in such works that his art is at its most mature and untrammelled.

If this is so, it may be asked, why did Chaucer make the Franklin say that he was repeating a Breton lay, rather than 'an old story'? There seem to be two reasons for this choice of imaginary source. One is connected with the character of the Franklin, as we have already seen it. He is devoted to the idea of *gentillesse*, but he is an elderly man and a country dweller, and it is therefore likely that he would be somewhat out of date in his notions of what was fashionable among the *gentil*. He begins, in flat defiance of the Host's 'Strawe for youre gentillesse!', by referring to 'Thise olde *gentil* Britouns', but what evidence there is suggests that the Breton lay was no longer a fashionable genre in the late fourteenth century. 'Thise olde Britouns' had once been *gentil*, but they were so no longer in Chaucer's time. He is deliberately making the Franklin choose a genre that has lost its vogue, just as he gives himself, as pilgrim, an antiquated tail-rhyme romance to tell. The second reason for this claim to a source is connected with the actual setting of the Tale. One of the great imaginative foci of the Tale, and particularly of its first half, is the black rocks, which are not known to derive from any source. It is these rocks that are the focus of Dorigen's anxiety during her husband's absence; this suggests to her the idea of setting the removal of the rocks as an impossible task to Aurelius; and this in turn is what introduces the important element of magic into the story. Now a chain of black rocks really is to be found off the Breton coast, and it may well have been this fact (learnt from charts, or from the conversation of some of the many Englishmen who had visited Brittany, or even conceivably from personal experience) that first gave

Chaucer the idea of a Breton setting for *The Franklin's Tale*. He then proceeded to fill in this setting with remarkably accurate topographical detail. Arveragus and his wife are said to live at *Pedmark*, and this is a real place, now called Penmarc'h, which is situated in Brittany south of Brest. It is now a small village, but in the fourteenth century it was a wealthy town, where aristocratic people such as Arveragus and Dorigen might well have lived. Penmarc'h is on a headland, and this headland really is surrounded by a chain of dark-coloured and dangerous rocks such as those mentioned in the poem. Even more surprising, Chaucer seems to have known how high the spring tides were on this part of the Breton coast, because he makes Aurelius pray (lines 387–9) that the flood tide should be so high that it is at least five fathoms (thirty feet) above the rocks. The mean range of the spring tides at this point is in fact such that if the flood tide were as high as this, then the ebb tide would still cover the rocks with a little to spare.[1] Other details in the Tale are equally accurate. Arveragus is said to come from *Kayrrud*, which seems to be a phonetic spelling of a genuine fourteenth-century Breton place-name. Aurelius's brother has been a student at Orleans university, where he saw a book of natural magic belonging to a fellow-student who was supposed to be studying law. In the Middle Ages young Bretons really did go to Orleans to study, and it really was a great centre of legal studies. The Breton background to the story is thus remarkably full and coherent. Paradoxically, this very fact is a further reason why *The Franklin's Tale* is unlike a Breton lay. The genuine lays are quite lacking in topographical detail—their world is a vaguely imagined fairyland, where specific features such as the sea, castles, woods, and so on, appear and disappear as needed. The world of *The Franklin's Tale*, though it includes magic, is imagined with a solidity which is distinctively Chaucerian.

RHETORIC IN THE PROLOGUE

After the Franklin has supplied his misleading information about the origin of the subject-matter of his Tale, he continues his preface by saying something about its style. We shall find this to be equally misleading. What he says is:

[1] This intriguing piece of information is supplied by Professor Phyllis Hodgson in her edition of *The Franklin's Tale*.

> But sires, by cause I am a burel man,
> At my biginning first I yow biseche,
> Have me excused of my rude speche.
> I lerned nevere rethorik, certeyn;
> Thing that I speke, it moot be bare and pleyn.
> I sleep nevere on the Mount of Pernaso,
> Ne lerned Marcus Tullius Scithero.
> Colours ne knowe I none, withouten drede,
> But swiche colours as growen in the mede,
> Or elles swiche as men dye or peynte.
> Colours of rethorik been to me queynte;
> My spirit feeleth noght of swich mateere.
> But if yow list, my tale shul ye heere.   (44–56)

We have seen how the Franklin has connected *eloquence* with *gentillesse*, and these modest remarks about the lack of *rethorik* to be expected in his Tale are perfectly in keeping with his unease about his social position. He began by putting the Squire firmly in his place; then he rushed to the other extreme and showed excessive deference to the *cherlissh* Host; now he continues with his excessive modesty, saying that he is *burel* (plain), so that his speech will naturally be *rude* (unpolished). But to begin a literary work in this way, with an apology for one's own incapacity, is in fact a part of *rethorik*: it is a device called *diminutio*, which medieval writers on rhetoric recommend as a way of capturing one's audience's sympathy. Thus, even in denying that he knows anything of rhetoric, the Franklin is displaying his acquaintance with it. The modesty of his preface can only be mock-modesty, a concealed form of ostentation. Once we recognize this, we shall find that it is so in detail throughout the lines just quoted; but, before we examine them more closely, a few words must be said about the nature of the *rethorik* of which the Franklin claims to know nothing.[1]

Rhetoric was one of the 'seven liberal arts' on which medieval education was based. It contained three branches, the art of preaching (*ars praedicandi*), the art of letter-writing (*ars dictaminis*), and the art of poetry (*ars poetica*). It is the last to which the Franklin is referring as *rethorik*. There exist a number of medieval elementary textbooks on the art of poetry (*artes*

---

[1] For a fuller account of Chaucer's rhetoric, see *An Introduction to Chaucer*, pp. 102–14.

poeticae), from some of which Chaucer may well have been taught at school. He mentions the author of one of them, Geoffroi de Vinsauf, and parodies a passage from his work, in *The Nun's Priest's Tale*. The *artes poeticae* conceive of poetry as essentially a matter of stylistic technique. They assume that the basic subject-matter of the poem (story, case to be argued, or whatever it is) will be supplied from outside, and that the poet's task is to embellish it as far as possible. This embellishment will normally consist of amplification—this indeed is what the Franklin assumes when he says that because he knows nothing of rhetoric his Tale will be *bare and pleyn*. The chief aim of the *artes poeticae* is to list and exemplify the various devices by which an amplifying embellishment may be carried out, devices which range from large-scale reorganizations of the narrative order, through the insertion of digressions of various kinds, down to the minute verbal details of style. Medieval rhetoric is thus a technique of a narrow kind, and one that has very little to say about the larger purposes which its devices may serve; but it could be learned thoroughly at an elementary level by poets and their audiences, and could then be used, often with conscious virtuosity, as an aid to expression. It is, of course, 'artificial'; but in the Middle Ages no one would have thought that nature was best expressed by natural means. Rhetoric is not sufficient in itself to make great poetry—no technique is; but Chaucer's works are sufficient testimony that great poetry can be made with the help of rhetoric.

Having said this, we can now return to *The Franklin's Prologue*. In line 48 he says that he can only be bare and plain in style, but in the next six lines he immediately goes on to repeat himself in an elaborately figurative manner. This trick of repeating the same ideas several times in different words is called by the *artes poeticae expolitio* or *interpretatio*. In line 49 he says that he has never slept on Mount Parnassus, a turn of phrase which is imitated from the Roman poet Persius (and thereby displays the Franklin's knowledge of classical poetry), and which is a roundabout way of saying that he is unacquainted with the Muses, the patron deities of poetry and the other arts, Parnassus being their home. This roundabout form of statement is recognized by the *artes poeticae* as *circumlocutio*. The next line is another example of *circumlocutio*, *Scithero* standing for rhetoric, since the famous Latin orator Cicero was the author of a number of works on rhetoric, and also had attributed to him in the Middle Ages the *Rhetorica ad Herennium* (now not thought to be by him), which was one of the main sources of the medieval *ars poetica*. Here then the Franklin is once more obliquely displaying his classical learning while seeming to deny it. In lines 51–4 he says that he knows nothing of the colours of rhetoric (*colours* being the technical name for stylistic embellishments), but only of the straightforward colours of the flowers or of the dyer or painter. This sounds like a *burel man* speaking; yet the pun on *colour* is itself a rhetorical device, called *adnominatio*; and, more than this, the idea of 'flowers of rhetoric' was a traditional one in learned medieval Latin poetry, while the analogy between poetry and painting had a respectable classical ancestry, going at least as far back as Horace's *Art of Poetry*. Yet again the Franklin is covertly displaying his learning in the very words in which he says what an ignorant fellow he is. His whole passage about rhetoric is a masterpiece of rhetorical trickery, and there can be no doubt that we are intended to notice this and to notice the contrast between what the Franklin professes and what he does even while professing it. In the first place, the passage is a display of virtuosity on Chaucer's part, which his audience would have recognized and enjoyed as such. Secondly, for the Franklin, it is a means by which, while modestly and politely claiming to be ignorant, he can disclose to the more judicious among the pilgrims that he is really skilled in rhetoric and in classical learning generally. And thirdly, for Chaucer and for us, it exposes an ostentation in his modesty which prevents him from being truly *gentil*.

RHETORIC IN THE TALE

Once we have seen the various depths of significance in this passage about rhetoric in *The Franklin's Prologue*, we shall be prepared to find something more than simplicity in the Franklin's use of rhetoric in the Tale. Certainly we shall not expect that what he says will really be *bare and pleyn*, devoid of rhetorical colouring. *The Franklin's Tale* makes use of all the usual rhetorical devices that are found in Chaucer. Some of these are part of the common technique of medieval poetry, and there is no particular reason for connecting them with the Franklin. One might mention, for example, the digression or *diversio* of lines 89–114.

Here, having described the unusual marriage relationship agreed on by Arveragus and Dorigen, the Franklin turns aside to give his own views of marriage—

> For o thing, sires, saufly dar I seye

—and then returns to this particular marriage to show how it exemplifies his own ideal. Digression is encouraged by the *artes poeticae* as a means of amplifying a given story, and Chaucer frequently uses it in *The Canterbury Tales* as a means of bringing out explicitly a theme that will emerge from the story he is telling. Or, to turn to smaller devices, lines 101–3 within this *diversio* form the kind of generalizing statement about life that is called a *sententia*:

> Pacience is an heigh vertu, certeyn,
> For it venquisseth, as thise clerkes seyn,
> Thinges that rigour sholde nevere atteyne.

Sententiae are very common in Chaucer's poetry and in medieval poetry in general, for medieval writers normally prefer to draw an explicit moral for themselves, or to support a particular incident by quoting a proverbial generalization, rather than leave it to their audiences to learn the lesson or supply the reason. Since most medieval poetry was written to be read aloud, the *artes poeticae* are much concerned with the auditory patterning of literature, and particularly with the repetition of words and phrases in different parts of sentences. The repetition of a word at the beginning of a series of sentences, for instance, is called *repetitio*, and we find an effective example of this in *The Franklin's Tale* in Aurelius's brother's recollection of the different wonders that have been performed by magicians:

> Somtime hath semed come a grim leoun;
> And somtime floures springe as in a mede;
> Somtime a vine, and grapes white and rede;
> Somtime a castel, al of lym and stoon.   (474–7)

There would be no point in exemplifying further the use of such common rhetorical devices in *The Franklin's Tale*. They are part of the normal machinery and idiom of Chaucerian poetry, and there is no reason why any of them should be called to our attention. But there are at least two rhetorical devices in the poem which stand out as rather unusual, and which seem to have some connexion with the Franklin's remarks about rhetoric in his Prologue. One of these is the description of nightfall after Dorigen has set Aurelius his seemingly impossible task:

> But sodeynly bigonne revel newe
> Til that the brighte sonne loste his hewe;
> For th'orisonte hath reft the sonne his light—
> This is as muche to seye as it was night.　　(343–6)

These lines form a periphrasis or *circumlocutio*, a device recommended by the *artes poeticae*, but learnt by Chaucer, in this particular form of an astronomical periphrasis for a time or season, from Italian poetry, particularly perhaps from the *Divine Comedy* of Dante and the *Teseida* of Boccaccio. The addition of the last line, however, makes the device into a particularly ostentatious sign of the Franklin's knowledge of rhetoric, because it explains what the periphrasis means in straightforward language. This explanation is very much in keeping with the Franklin's comments on rhetoric in his Prologue, and it shares their multiple significance. From one point of view it is a *burel man*'s humorously deflating comment on the pretensions of rhetoric, but from another point of view it exactly reproduces the language of the *artes poeticae* themselves in commenting on other poets' use of *circumlocutio*. Thus Geoffroi de Vinsauf, the rhetorician mentioned in *The Nun's Priest's Tale*, writes as follows of the opening lines of Virgil's *Aeneid*: 'Virgil gives a *circumlocutio* for Aeneas: "I sing of arms and of the man who first sailed from the land of Troy to Italy and came to its Lavinian shore". This is as much to say as "I will write about Aeneas".' So once again the Franklin is displaying his knowledge of rhetoric even while pretending to ignorance.

The second unusual and apparently 'Franklinesque' example of rhetoric is a much longer and more elaborate one. It occurs in the lament of Dorigen after Aurelius has told her that the rocks have disappeared, so that she is obliged to become his mistress. She argues that many virgins and many wives have committed suicide rather than be dishonoured, and she supports this argument with a list (lines 695–784) of no fewer than twenty-two examples of women who have done just that. The lament, or *exclamatio*, is a common enough device of medieval rhetoric, and so is the *exemplum*, or illustration of some general principle by reference to a particular story from life or literature. But such an enormous list of *exempla* is quite out of the ordinary, and, even when we allow for the change of taste between Chaucer's time and ours, it is difficult to believe that it can be intended to be taken exactly at face value. Its length seems to be carefully calculated. All of the *exempla* are taken from a single source, the *Adversus Jovinianum* of St Jerome, a major source of medieval writings in favour of virginity and against marriage. But they do not occur in the same order in Jerome as they do in Chaucer, and Chaucer's order seems to suggest that he went through the *Adversus Jovinianum* at least twice. The first time he selected *exempla* with care, classified them (see lines 723–6), told them at length, and then came to what appears intended as a conclusion (see lines 747–53). The second time he was determined to lengthen the original list, made use of all conceivably usable material, and told the stories only briefly or allusively. This suggests that he was deliberately intending to turn the list into an ostentatious display of rhetoric, comparable on a much larger scale with the self-conscious astronomical *circumlocutio* we have just been looking at, and giving the lie to the 'I lerned nevere rethorik, certeyn' of *The Franklin's Prologue*. However, this display of rhetoric can scarcely be simply a bit of fun at the Franklin's expense, or at the expense of rhetoric itself; if it is a joke of this kind, it goes on far too long. I shall argue later that it also has a point to make about Dorigen, of characteristically Chaucerian slyness.[1] This is undoubtedly its most important function in *The Franklin's Tale* as a whole, but I suspect that it was originally suggested to Chaucer by his conception of the Franklin as secretly proud of his skill in the *gentil* art of rhetoric.

THE FRANKLIN'S PURPOSE IN HIS TALE

We can now turn from *The Franklin's Prologue* to the Tale itself. There will be no question, of course, of submitting the whole of the Tale to the kind of close scrutiny that the Prologue has just undergone—the Tale is too long, and in any case most of it does not possess the richness of implication that we have found in the Prologue. In the Prologue the Franklin himself has been revealed; the Tale is of interest as a tale, and not merely as a further revelation of the Franklin. But it remains, and most distinctly, the *Franklin's* tale. He tells it to serve certain purposes of his

[1] See below, pp. 45–6.

own; and though, as I shall argue, it in fact escapes from those
purposes without his being aware of it, we must begin by con-
sidering what they are.

The Franklin intends his tale to be a moral fable, or, to see
it in medieval terms, to be an *exemplum* which proves certain
general moral principles. The Tale possesses three main themes:
that of *trouthe*, that of the ideal marriage relationship, and that
of *gentillesse*. On each of these themes the Franklin has definite
moral teaching to offer, teaching which is not allowed to remain
implicit and affect us through our imaginations alone, but which
is rendered explicit in the form of aphorisms or *sententiae*, to
which we are expected to give our rational assent. His teaching
on the subject of *trouthe* is the statement wrung out of Arveragus
in the agonizing moment when his wife tells him that Aurelius
has succeeded in performing the task which she swore would
win her love, and leaves it to him to decide what to do: 'Trouthe
is the hyeste thing that man may kepe' (807). On the subject of
marriage, his teaching is contained in his own remarks in the
digression suggested by the marriage agreement of Dorigen and
Arveragus. These form a whole series of *sententiae*, but perhaps
their quintessence may be found in the opening lines of the
digression:

> For o thing, sires, saufly dar I seye,
> That freendes everich oother moot obeye,
> If they wol longe holden compaignye.
> Love wol nat been constreyned by maistrye. (89–92)

The last line in particular seems to deserve to have next to it
the little pointing hand in the margin that in old texts sometimes
indicates the explicit teaching of a work. The third theme of
gentillesse is one on which emphasis is laid at various points
throughout the Tale, but we may find the Franklin's doctrine
summed up in the remarks made by Aurelius and the Clerk
when each of them decides not to demand fulfilment of a
promise:

> Thus kan a squier doon a gentil dede
> As wel as kan a knight, withouten drede (871–2)

and

> Thou art a squier and he is a knight;
> But God forbede, for his blisful might,
> But if a clerk koude doon a gentil dede
> As wel as any of yow, it is no drede! (937–40)

Gentillesse is not a matter of rank, but a virtue of spirit belonging to the individual. All this seems clear enough, and if his Tale were what the Franklin evidently intends it to be, it would serve merely to demonstrate the truth of these doctrines; though it would be somewhat surprising to find a single *exemplum* proving three such different morals. But when we come to examine each of the three themes in more detail as it is embodied in the actual Tale, we shall find that the matter is less simple than it seems. In each case, the theme will be found to point not towards the clarity of an *exemplum*, but towards ambiguity and dubiety— qualities which are more troubling than simplicity and clarity, but also more interesting and more like life. Let us consider each of the themes separately.

Trouthe

The concept of *trouthe*, meaning 'fidelity to one's pledged word', is certainly a central theme in *The Franklin's Tale*, and one that reflects the legal knowledge and interests that *The General Prologue* portrait implied in the Franklin. The suspense that the narrative generates turns on two promises: Dorigen's promise to Aurelius that she will be his if he removes the rocks from the Breton coast, and Aurelius's promise to the Clerk that he will pay him a thousand pounds if he makes it appear that this has been done. *Trouthe* is invoked when both promises are given: Dorigen says

> Thanne wol I love yow best of any man,
> Have heer my trouthe, in al that evere I kan,   (325–6)

while Aurelius declares

> This bargain is ful drive, for we been knit.
> Ye shal be payed trewely, by my trouthe!   (558–9)

The promises thus given are treated as formal and legally binding contracts, and when, through the influence of *gentillesse*, Aurelius releases Dorigen and is in turn released by the Clerk, the releases are performed with due formality and in language which recalls that actually used in legal 'quitclaims' of the Middle Ages. Aurelius says to Dorigen

> I yow relesse, madame, into youre hond
> Quit every serement and every bond
> That ye han maad to me as heerbiforn,
> Sith thilke time which that ye were born,   (861–4)

even though she has given him no written oaths or agreements which he could return to her and she has made him only one promise since she was born. But medieval quitclaims tended to include some such phrase as *a principio mundi usque in diem presencium* ('from the beginning of the world down to this present day'). Similarly, the Clerk says formally to Aurelius 'I release you' and invents a slightly comic parody of the intensifying phrase to go with it:

> Sire, I releesse thee thy thousand pound,
> As thou right now were cropen out of the ground,
> Ne nevere er now ne haddest knowen me.   (941–3)

The most important invocation of *trouthe*, however, occurs at the point just mentioned, when Arveragus becomes the fourth of the Tale's four central characters to get involved with the theme. Dorigen has promised to love Aurelius if he can perform the apparently impossible task of removing the black rocks which she sees as a danger to her husband. Aurelius tells her that the deed has been done, demands the fulfilment of her promise, and as he does so warns her

> Aviseth yow er that ye breke youre trouthe.   (648)

She takes the dilemma to her husband, and he tells her that she must keep her promise, because 'Trouthe is the hyeste thing that man may kepe'. We might well dismiss the incident out of hand by referring it to the Franklin's own legalistic cast of mind. Who but a lawyer or the creature of a lawyer's imagination would think of forcing his wife to keep a frivolous verbal promise to become another man's mistress on condition that he performed a deed which she believed to be impossible? Indeed, the Franklin himself recognizes the oddity of Arveragus's decision, and anticipates protests from his listeners:

> Paraventure an heep of yow, ywis,
> Wol holden him a lewed man in this
> That he wol putte his wyf in jupartie.   (821–3)

If, however, we respond to the human drama of the situation as Chaucer presents it, we shall find that we cannot dismiss it so easily. Arveragus's *sententia* does not come out pat, as the conclusion of a complacent statement of general principle. It is the last line of a speech in which he is desperately trying to rouse his wife from her misery, by not letting her see his own agony of mind. But as he pronounces the *sententia*, his agony breaks through, and 'with that word he brast anon to wepe' (808). He is stretched on the rack of his own principle, and the dramatic moment has an intensity which gives the principle itself a searing force. Once we begin to take the principle seriously, though, a question immediately forces itself on us. What about Dorigen's original marriage promise to Arveragus, in the making of which *trouthe* was also invoked?—

> Sire, I wol be youre humble trewe wyf,
> Have heer my trouthe, til that myn herte breste.   (86–7)

Trouthe may be *the hyeste thing that man may kepe*, but it seems that Arveragus can only make his wife keep her *trouthe* to Aurelius by forcing her to break her *trouthe* to himself. Surely her original marriage pledge has priority and should invalidate the later promise to Aurelius? We ask such questions in vain. They clearly did not occur to the Franklin, and, though they must have occurred to Chaucer, because the theme of *trouthe* is so carefully repeated throughout the Tale, one might well suggest that he did not intend them to occur to his audience. I have argued, however, that it is the very intensity of the human situation from which the *sententia* emerges that forces us to take it seriously and consider all its implications. If we do so, we are surely left with a genuine question—genuine in the sense that no single answer is provided or implied in the Tale—but we are left free to argue about the matter after the Tale has ended. And the fact that the Tale ends with an explicit question about *gentillesse* suggests that it may imply questions about its other themes too.

Marriage

The second theme of *The Franklin's Tale* is that of marriage. This is in a way an intrusive topic, which the Franklin seems to be imposing on the Tale because it relates to interests of his own. The popular story from which the Tale is derived, the story of how the heroine escaped from the consequences of her foolish promise, does not require any special emphasis on the ideal quality of her relationship with her husband. We need to know that they truly love each other, certainly, or else his insistence that she should keep her promise would lose all dramatic force; but nothing more than this is strictly necessary. The Franklin, however, is determined to include more than this, and so he explains at some length the unusual agreement they come to about their relationship, and then turns aside in the *diversio* we have already mentioned to defend this arrangement on grounds of general principle. The arrangement is that, instead of Arveragus's taking on the dominance (*maistrie*) that usually belonged to the medieval husband, he agrees to obey Dorigen in everything as a medieval lover was expected to obey his mistress. In return, she agrees to obey him, and so each of them becomes servant and each of them master. The defence of this arrangement is that 'Love is a thing as any spirit free' (95), and hence 'wol nat been constreyned by maistrye' (92). And so it is best for married lovers to be not domineering but patient. During the present century, at least, most readers of *The Franklin's Tale* seem to have shared this view of the marriage relationship in the poem, and to have felt that it was Chaucer's own view (which would certainly explain why it is so much insisted on), and that it was presented as the conclusion to a debate on the subject of marriage that was embodied in a number of the other *Canterbury Tales*. These opinions cannot, however, be taken for granted, but must be examined more closely.

The idea that a debate or discussion on marriage is embodied in parts of *The Canterbury Tales* was first put forward by G. L. Kittredge in 1912.[1] It quickly achieved general acceptance, and a reliable more recent survey of the subject can be found in W. W. Lawrence's book *Chaucer and the Canterbury Tales*.[2] The core of the debate is to be found in four tales, those of the Wife of Bath, the Clerk, the Merchant, and the Franklin. Although the manuscripts of *The Canterbury Tales* arrange the various fragments that have come down to us in different orders, there is general agreement that these four tales are intended to follow in the order given. They are all concerned not simply with marriage, but with the question of *maistrie* or dominance in marriage, a favourite topic of both learned and popular discussion in the Middle Ages. The Wife of Bath is an extreme example of the dominance of the wife. She explains in her long Prologue how she has had five husbands in her long life and has achieved *maistrie* over all of them, and she then tells a tale in which a knight has imposed on him the task of discovering what

[1] See p. 1, n. 1.
[2] Oxford University Press, 1950. See ch. 5.

thing it is that women most desire. He is given the right answer —*maistrie* or *sovereignetee*—by an ugly old woman, but only on condition that he marries her. He is disgusted by her ugliness and ignoble birth, but, after she has lectured him at length on the subject of *gentillesse*, he concedes *maistrie* to her, and she at once turns by magic into a young, beautiful, and obedient wife. After *The Wife of Bath's Tale* there follow the tales of the Friar and the Summoner, which are not concerned with marriage, but the subject is then taken up again by the Clerk. He tells a story of a peasant girl who is married to a marquis; he submits her to an incredible series of torments and humiliations, all of which she accepts patiently, and at last, when he finds how obedient she is, takes her back into favour. The Clerk says that he tells this tale as a parable showing how we should all bear the tests God sends to us, but he makes specific reference to the Wife of Bath, and to the difference between her heroine and his. *The Merchant's Tale* comes next, and this is explicitly linked with *The Clerk's Tale*. The Merchant has recently married a wife who is the very opposite of the Clerk's patient heroine, and he tells a story of an old knight who marries a young girl after a lifetime of bachelor dissipation, and is at once deceived by her. He is struck blind, and she commits adultery with a young squire in a garden in her husband's very presence.

It will be clear at once that there exist close and complex links between *The Franklin's Tale* and the three tales just summarized. In the first place, the Franklin seems to offer a halfway house between the two extremes represented by the Wife of Bath and the Clerk: neither total dominance by the wife nor total dominance by the husband, but a compromise in which both are master and both servant. Moreover, the Franklin seems to be defending marriage itself against the cynicism of the Merchant's attack, by repeating the basic situation of his Tale—the marriage of a knight and a lady subverted by the advances of a young squire—but bringing it to an unironically happy conclusion, in which the marriage remains intact, but even the squire does not suffer too much. Again, in linking *gentillesse* with marriage as the subjects of his Tale, the Franklin is not merely influenced by the Squire (whose tale comes as an interlude in the marriage debate, between the Merchant and the Franklin), but is returning to *The Wife of Bath's Tale*, where the knight had to learn the nature of true *gentillesse* before he could find happiness by conceding *maistrie*

to his wife. There are even certain more detailed links between
The Franklin's Tale and the earlier contributions to the debate.
The twenty-two *exempla* of Dorigen's lament are all taken from
St Jerome's *Adversus Jovinianum*, a book from which many of
the Wife of Bath's arguments in her Prologue are borrowed, and
which was included in the collection of anti-feminist writings
which her fifth husband was in the habit of reading. And certain
lines in the Franklin's remarks about marriage seem to echo
deliberately remarks of the Merchant. Compare the Merchant's

> How mighte a man han any adversitee
> That hath a wif? Certes, I kan nat seye.
> The blisse which that is bitwixe hem tweye
> Ther may no tonge telle, or herte thinke

with the Franklin's

> Who koude telle, but he hadde wedded be,
> The joye, the ese, and the prosperitee
> That is bitwixe an housbonde and his wyf?
> A yeer and moore lasted this blisful lyf. (131–4)

There are echoes both in the language used and in the interrogative form of the statements. The Merchant's rhetorical
question was spoken with bitter sarcasm, but the Franklin chal-
lengingly repeats it in a literal sense, wishing to substitute for
the Merchant's cynicism a more idealistic view of marriage.

It does not follow from this, however, that Chaucer intended
The Franklin's Tale as a solution to the problem of *maistrie* in
marriage raised by the earlier tales. In general, Chaucer is not
in the habit of offering solutions to problems; his tendency rather
is to present human situations as they are (which includes pre-
senting them as moral situations) and to leave us to draw our
own conclusions. Let us examine what the Franklin is trying to
do in his initial treatment of the marriage relationship of Arveragus and Dorigen. He begins with a situation typical of the
kind of chivalric literature to which Breton lays belonged.
A knight loves a beautiful lady from a distance; he performs
many services to win her; she takes *pitee* on his *penaunce*; and
at last she agrees to marry him. So far their relationship has
belonged to the convention of *fine amour*, by which the lady is
the dominant partner (the knight's 'mistress' in a literal sense)

and her lover is subservient. But this relationship must end with marriage, once the lady has conceded that, for in medieval marriage the husband is dominant. This at least was the medieval theory, though in practice there were of course always Wives of Bath, who had the personal power to reverse this normal order. But in this particular marriage, a completely unusual arrangement is tried. Arveragus promises to go on behaving as a lover; he will 'hire obeye, and folwe hir wil in al' (77), though this situation will be concealed from the outside world. In return Dorigen promises to be his 'humble trewe wyf' (86) none the less; so that what is intended is clearly a combination of, or compromise between, the two radically opposed relationships of lover and mistress and husband and wife. At this point the Franklin begins on his *diversio* in defence and explanation of their agreement. The gist of his remarks lies, as I have said, in the *sententia* 'Love wol not been constreyned by maistrye' (92). The 'debate' about marriage among the pilgrims has been a debate about *maistrie* in marriage. Both sides have agreed that marriage is to be seen as a struggle for power, in which either husband or wife must come out victorious. The Franklin wants to resolve the problem by changing its terms; he wishes to remove the whole question of dominance from marriage, and to present it as something other than a power relationship. Women by nature desire liberty, he argues; so do men;[1] therefore both parties to a marriage must show *pacience* and *suffrance*. Most modern readers, at least in Western Europe and the English-speaking countries, are likely to feel that the Franklin is right about this. We believe that husband and wife should be equal partners in all respects, and that power should have nothing to do with the matter. It is not at all certain, however, that this would be the medieval reaction. The normal medieval view was that a happy marriage relationship would be established, not by trying to get ride of the element of dominance completely, but by both parties agreeing that the husband should be dominant. The natural relationship was as stated in a standard medieval encyclopaedic work, the *De Proprietatibus Rerum* of Bartholomew the Englishman: 'A man is the hede of a woman, as the appostle sayth. And therefore a

[1] In the 13th century French *Roman de la Rose*, a seminal work for Chaucer, the character called *La Vieille* (the Old Woman) argues that Nature makes women desire liberty; but the irony with which her teaching is surrounded implies that men and women should follow a higher law than Nature's.

man is bounde to rule his wyfe, as the heed hath cure and rule of the body.'[1] What Arveragus and Dorigen are trying to do, though their intentions (and the Franklin's) are no doubt good, is to upset the ordained order of things. This fact is already reflected perhaps in the confused way in which the Franklin defines their relationship. He tries to get rid of *maistrie*, but only loses himself in paradoxes in which *maistrie* seems to reappear constantly whether he wishes so or not. Thus when he praises patience, it is only as a way of achieving *maistrie* indirectly:

> Looke who that is moost pacient in love,
> He is at his avantage al above.
> Pacience is an heigh vertu, certeyn,
> For it venquisseth, as thise clerkes seyn,
> Thinges that rigour sholde nevere atteyne.   (99–103)

And the Franklin's final statement of their relationship is in terms of a further knot of paradoxes:

> Thus hath she take hir servant and hir lord—
> Servant in love, and lord in mariage.
> Thanne was he bothe in lordshipe and servage.
> Servage? nay, but in lordshipe above...   (120–3)

Only in a transcendental world where opposites become one would such an intensity of paradox escape from its own terms of mastery and servitude. But this marriage, like others, has to manage as best it can in the real world.

What happens to the marriage of Dorigen and Arveragus when it is tested by the course of the story appears to demonstrate the confusion and impracticability of the Franklin's ideal. This is quite the contrary of what the Franklin seems to intend, but the story has a human life that frees it from his exemplifying intentions. There can be no doubt of Dorigen's depth of affection for her husband, and she is thoroughly shocked when, in his absence, Aurelius says that he loves her. Nevertheless, she mitigates the force of her refusal by telling Aurelius that if he removes the rocks from the coast of Brittany she will love him in return. In this incident, we are perhaps to see her as acting in accordance with the confused ideals the Franklin has stated:

[1] This is from the fourteenth-century translation by John of Trevisa, book 4, ch. 14. The same doctrine is put forward in Chaucer's *Parson's Tale*, which takes the form of a sermon. The doctrine goes back to St Paul, 1st Epistle to the Corinthians, xi. 3, and Epistle to the Ephesians, v. 22 ff.

though she is a wife, and has the appropriate feelings, she continues to act as a courtly mistress, setting her suitor a difficult task to perform as the condition of gaining her *pitee*. With the aid of magic, he performs the task, and Dorigen is now in a terrible dilemma. She considers suicide, but at this point her husband returns, and she immediately takes her problem to him. Just as this is a crucial point in the tale so far as the theme of *trouthe* is concerned, so it is with the theme of marriage. In taking her problem to her husband, Dorigen has not acted in accordance with theory, which would evidently have led her to kill herself. She has acted instinctively, and instinct has led her to the submission that in the Middle Ages would have been thought appropriate for a wife. Arveragus in turn, under the pressure of this crisis, resumes his role as 'head' and instructs her what to do:

> Ye shul youre trouthe holden, by my fay!   (802)

(It is perhaps worth recalling that *shul* had a rather strong sense —nearer to 'must' than to the modern 'shall'.) Thus at this crucial point, *maistrie* re-enters the marriage, with an emphasis that gains force from the paradox by which Arveragus uses his *maistrie* to order his wife to keep her promise to become someone else's mistress. From this point on, the theme of *maistrie* in marriage is dropped, and *gentillesse* takes its place as the central theme of the closing stages of the Tale.

I ought perhaps to add that the question of marriage in *The Franklin's Tale* is more controversial than most other aspects of the Tale, and that the account just given of Chaucer's and the Franklin's intentions would by no means be universally accepted among medievalists. Many modern critics have felt sympathetic towards the Franklin's views on marriage, and, noting that the Franklin and Chaucer belonged to roughly the same social group, and had even held some of the same offices (president of the magistrates' court and knight of the shire), have felt that Chaucer was using him as the mouthpiece for his own views. This may of course be so, and it would be wrong to pretend to certainty in the matter. But it must be remembered that even (perhaps especially) on a topic of such central human interest as marriage, views that now seem enlightened might in the Middle Ages have seemed absurd, and vice versa; and one of the greatest dangers for those with a real admiration for a writer from the past is to be unable to bear to feel that they disagree with him on any important topic.

Introduction

Gentillesse

The third theme of *The Franklin's Tale* is *gentillesse*, and the Tale is better adapted to convey this theme than either of the others. We have seen that *gentillesse* is a topic with which the Franklin is much preoccupied in his Prologue, and that, despite the Host's contempt, he immediately introduces the word *gentil* into the first line of his prefatory remarks about Breton lays. We shall therefore expect the theme to recur in the body of the Tale. Once again the crucial point is the scene in which Dorigen takes her dilemma to her husband and he instructs her to keep her promise to Aurelius. In doing so, he is acting according to his conception of *trouthe*; he is also reasserting his *maistrie* in marriage; and thirdly this is the poem's first great act of *gentillesse*. So Aurelius sees it, when Dorigen goes to the garden to keep her promise:

> Madame, seyth to youre lord Arveragus
> That sith I se his grete gentillesse
> To yow...,
> I have wel levere evere to suffre wo
> Than I departe the love bitwix yow two.   (854–60)

Gentillesse is entirely appropriate to Arveragus, for he is a knight; but his *gentillesse* touches off a second *gentil* deed by Aurelius, a squire, and therefore lower in chivalric status. He releases Dorigen from her rash promise to him, saying

> Thus kan a squier doon a gentil dede
> As wel as kan a knight, withouten drede.   (871–2)

Aurelius in his turn goes to the Clerk to ask for time to pay. The Clerk is outside the order of chivalry entirely, and at first it seems that, like Shylock, he is going to demand fulfilment of the bond. 'Have I nat holden covenant unto thee?' (915), he asks, and again, 'Hastow nat had thy lady as thee liketh?' (917). To the first question the answer can only be 'Yes', but to the second it is a miserable 'No, no'. Aurelius explains what has happened:

> Arveragus, of gentillesse,
> Hadde levere die in sorwe and in distresse
> Than that his wyf were of hir trouthe fals.   (923–5)

33

He further explains what passed between himself and Dorigen:

> That made me han of hire so greet pitee;
> And right as frely as he sente hire me,
> As frely sente I hire to him ageyn.   (931–3)

The repeated word *frely*, with its sense hovering between 'freely' (applying to Dorigen) and 'generously' (applying to Arveragus and Aurelius), invokes a concept closely connected with *gentillesse*. *Franchise* (the noun from the adjective *fre*) is one aspect of *gentillesse*—the unselfregarding generosity that is necessary for truly *gentil* behaviour. It has been introduced a little earlier in the Tale, in close connexion with *gentillesse*, at the point where Aurelius is first confronted with Arveragus's *gentillesse* and Dorigen's misery, and decides

> That fro his lust yet were him levere abide
> Than doon so heigh a cherlissh wrecchednesse
> Agains franchise and alle gentillesse.   (850–2)

Now, confronted with the *franchise* to which Aurelius's *gentillesse* has led him, the Clerk decides that he too must be *gentil* and release Aurelius from his enormous debt. In doing so he says:

> Leeve brother,
> Everich of yow dide gentilly til oother.
> Thou art a squier and he is a knight;
> But God forbede, for his blisful might,
> But if a clerk koude doon a gentil dede
> As wel as any of yow, it is no drede!   (935–40)

He then rides away, and the story ends. The Franklin himself has the last word, directing the pilgrims' attention towards the ethical theme of *franchise*:

> Lordinges, this question, thanne, wol I aske now,
> Which was the mooste fre, as thinketh yow?   (949–50)

The Franklin's intentions with regard to *gentillesse* are quite clear, and he has been successful in carrying them out. We have seen that his own almost obsessive concern with *gentillesse* is connected with his unease about his relationship to the chivalric class and its virtues. He therefore tells a story which will act as an *exemplum* of *gentillesse*, so as to establish that it is a virtue whose nature he understands, but one which will as far as pos-

sible detach the virtue from its class associations. He therefore
shifts the emphasis towards the end of his Tale on to *franchise*,
an aspect of *gentillesse* which (unlike, say, exquisite manners) has
no necessary connexion with aristocratic birth and breeding.[1]
And so the Clerk, who has no chivalric status at all, can match
the knight and the squire in *gentillesse* by his generosity in the
matter of money. In the twentieth century we are likely to feel
that the Franklin is entirely right in thus locating the true value
of *gentillesse* in virtuous actions rather than in high birth, and
this time I think our feelings coincide with Chaucer's. This is
precisely the point he makes in his *ballade* called *Gentillesse*:

> What man that claimeth gentil for to be
> Must...alle his wittes dresse
> Vertu to sewe and vices for to flee.
> For unto vertu longeth dignitee,
> And noght the revers...

The point is also made by the ugly old woman in *The Wife of
Bath's Tale*. In *The Franklin's Tale* the second and third acts of
gentillesse are set off in a chain-reaction by the first and second
and, on a smaller scale, they release generosity in ourselves. The
conclusion of the Tale has a genuine, unequivocal warmth.

There remains, however, a certain equivocal quality in the
first act of *gentillesse*, which sparks off the others. It makes,
indeed, as dubious an *exemplum* of *gentillesse* as it does of *trouthe*
and of the avoidance of *maistrie* in marriage. The passage with
which Arveragus continues his instructions to Dorigen after his
sententia about *trouthe* is somewhat surprising:

> 'Trouthe is the hyeste thing that man may kepe'—
> But with that word he brast anon to wepe,
> And seyde, 'I yow forbede, up peyne of deeth,
> That nevere, whil thee lasteth lyf ne breeth,
> To no wight telle thou of this aventure—
> As I may best, I wol my wo endure—
> Ne make no contenance of hevinesse,
> That folk of yow may demen harm or gesse'.   (807–14)

It seems as though Arveragus's emotion is caused as much by
the thought of what people would say about *him* if they knew

---

[1] Note, too, that one kind of freedom (*libertee*, achieved by defiance
of law) is thus replaced by another kind (*franchise*, achieved by going
beyond law).

the truth as by his feeling for his wife. This is very natural, of course, and very probable, but somewhat odd as part of an exemplary demonstration of *gentillesse*. But it fits in very well with the Franklin's conception of *gentillesse*. We have seen him in his Prologue greatly concerned about social status and reputation, and, though he insists there on *vertu* as the essence of *gentillesse*, he shows a similar concern with reputation in his treatment of Arveragus at the very beginning of his Tale. Arveragus has agreed to take on himself no *maistrie* over Dorigen, and this is evidently from the Franklin's point of view an admirable arrangement, yet he seems to think it perfectly natural that Arveragus should not wish it to be publicly known, for his reputation's sake:

> Save that the name of soverainetee,
> That wolde he have for shame of his degree.   (79–80)

His later reaction to Dorigen's dilemma is perfectly in keeping with this. It is true, no doubt, that medieval aristocratic values did depend on external reputation to a greater extent than is likely to seem proper to modern readers; nevertheless, it is difficult not to feel that Chaucer intends us to see in Arveragus an all-too-human *approach* to *gentillesse*, which is taken by the Franklin for the thing itself, but is really somewhat less than that.

Certain other details in the Tale support this interpretation by laying an unexpected stress on reputation or social status. One of these is an afterthought, psychologically very convincing, at the end of the speech by Aurelius's brother in which he introduces the idea of removing the rocks by magic. If this could be done, he concludes,

> Thanne were my brother warisshed of his wo;
> Thanne moste she nedes holden hire biheste,
> Or elles he shal shame hire atte leeste.   (490–2)

Now it seems most unlikely that to humiliate Dorigen would give any satisfaction at all to a man so desperately in love with her as Aurelius is supposed to be. His brother, however, feels indignant at the suffering she is causing him, and would like to punish her for it, and the idea of *shame*, or public humiliation, as a punishment would naturally occur to the Franklin. A second detail occurs when Aurelius is wondering what he will do to pay the Clerk. He decides that he must sell his inheritance and beg for his living, but then he adds the thought that he will have to do it somewhere else so as not to shame his relations:

> ...heere may I nat dwelle,
> And shamen al my kinrede in this place.   (892–3)

Both of these details suggest thoughts which it would be perfectly natural for someone in the situation concerned to have, but they also help to build up a picture of an excessive and not perfectly *gentil* concern about reputation. *Gentillesse* and *shame*, though far from opposites, are perhaps not quite so closely connected as the Franklin feels, and it is worth noting that the very word *shame* occurs in both the passages just quoted, as it does in line 80 (quoted above), and in line 857 (with reference to the risk Arveragus runs in telling Dorigen to keep her promise to Aurelius).

From our examination of the Tale's three central themes of *trouthe*, the marriage relationship, and *gentillesse*, it has emerged that in all three cases there is some confusion or ambiguity in the Franklin's treatment of them, with the result that the Tale does not function perfectly as an *exemplum* of any of the three. From this it may sound as though the Tale ought to be considered a failure; but in fact the very reverse is true. The Franklin intends his Tale (it would appear) as a neat moral fable, a machine adapted to convey certain teaching in a clear and unambiguous form. This is not how the Tale turns out, but it is surely all the better for it. It is better than the Franklin intends or knows, because it shares some of the confusion and ambiguity of real life. The characters in *The Franklin's Tale*, though they begin as ideal types, behave under the pressure of events in a convincingly human (and therefore often unideal) way. They will not be imprisoned by the abstractions they are intended to convey; instead, they go their own ways, and convey a meaning that is more complex and richer than could have been predicted. The Franklin is not aware of this, but Chaucer of course is, and it is part of his intention that we should recognize the gaps between what the teller intends and what the tale conveys. The scheme of *The Canterbury Tales* as a whole is devised to make such subtleties possible; and indeed Chaucer throughout his poetic career had been working towards a freer and more relativistic employment of the narrator in his fictions.[1] From this point, however, we can largely leave the Franklin and his intentions behind, and go on to discuss the Chaucerian achievement of the Tale itself.

I have said that the Tale's characters begin as ideal types, and I think this is true of all four of them. Arveragus and Dorigen enter as noble knight and lady, he daring and she beautiful; Aurelius as a young squire, an accomplished courtier and extravagant lover; and the anonymous Clerk as a fairy-tale magician who displays his mysteriously gained knowledge from the very beginning:

> And after that he seyde a wonder thing:
> 'I knowe,' quod he, 'the cause of youre coming.'
> And er they ferther any foote wente,
> He tolde hem al that was in hire entente.   (503–6)

The characters begin, that is, by being like those of *The Knight's Tale* or *The Squire's Tale*, examples of the chivalric literature that the Franklin admires and wishes to imitate. When they enter, we are interested in them not as persons but as units in a familiar pattern, symbolic of general feelings and ideas, and at a far distance from the complexities of our everyday lives. Conventional characterization of this type is most fully developed in the case of Aurelius, and it will be worth examining the way in which he is presented in a little more detail.

Aurelius

Aurelius is first mentioned as dancing among those friends of Dorigen who are trying to cheer her up in her husband's absence. He is described at once in a leisurely and formal way, which corresponds to the *descriptio* recommended by the *artes poeticae* as a means of amplification:

> Daunced a squier biforn Dorigen,
> That fressher was and jolier of array,

[1] I have developed this view in greater detail in *An Introduction to Chaucer*, ch. 4.

As to my doom, than is the month of May.
He singeth, daunceth, passinge any man
That is, or was, sith that the world bigan.
Therwith he was, if men sholde him discrive,
Oon of the beste faringe man on live;
Yong, strong, right vertuous, and riche, and wys,
And wel biloved, and holden in greet prys.   (254–62)

The description is in superlative terms, and it does not aim to individualize Aurelius but to classify him—he is everything that a young courtier ought to be. The comparison of him to the month of May is significant: he becomes a symbol of the season of youth and love. It has been pointed out that the description of Aurelius is very similar to that of the Squire in *The General Prologue*, particularly in that the May comparison is used there too:

He was as fressh as is the month of May.

But there is no reason to suppose, as has been suggested by some scholars, that the similarity is intended as a compliment to the Squire by the Franklin. It would scarcely be an unmixed compliment, for Aurelius at once sets himself to break up Dorigen's happy marriage; but in any case, the May image is part of the literary convention to which the descriptions of both squires belong. It is common in medieval poetry, and may sometimes be used of the courtly mistress as well as of her lover; thus Emelye in *The Knight's Tale* is 'fressher than the May'. Aurelius, then, is a thoroughly and deliberately conventional figure, a symbol rather than a person. It is in accordance with the convention that he should fall in love with Dorigen, and that his love should be of the extremest possible kind. In medieval courtly literature, the state of mind of the unaccepted lover is always one of intense misery, of *penaunce*. All the desire comes from his side; the lady is merely the passive (and sometimes ignorant) object of it, and if she eventually offers her *pitee* for his *penaunce*, it is, like the grace of the Christian God, as an uncovenanted favour, not as the reward for desert. The suffering of the lover according to this courtly convention was sketched in in the case of Arveragus before his suit was accepted by Dorigen; now, in the case of Aurelius, it is developed more fully. He does not dare to speak to her, and can only disclose his love obliquely in songs, 'as in a general compleyning' (273). He falls into despair, 'langwissheth as a furye dooth in helle' (278), and says he will die. At last he plucks up courage to declare his love to Dorigen, with the unhappy result that we have seen. Now his *penaunce* is redoubled. He feels death coming upon him fast:

> He seeth he may nat fro his deeth asterte;
> Him semed that he felte his herte colde.   (350–1)

He falls into a delirium, and makes an insane prayer to Apollo, asking the god to request his sister, Lucina the moon-goddess, to cause an unusually high spring tide to cover the rocks, and, by retarding her own rotation round the earth, to make it remain in being for two years. The conventional, non-realistic quality of the treatment of Aurelius is particularly striking in this speech. We are told that he prayed *in his raving* (354) and that *he niste what he spak* (356), yet Chaucer makes no attempt to introduce any note of delirium into the manner of the speech. It is a long and carefully constructed prayer, lucid in argument and elaborate in syntax, stating exactly the mythological and scientific basis for his request. It is evidently more important that the reasoning should be clear and that the speech should be a well-organized *pleynt* than that Aurelius's *raving* should be realistically imitated. The science of the prayer is mistaken, however (mistaken, that is, according to the geocentric medieval cosmology accepted by Chaucer). Even if Lucina did perform the *miracle* of revolving round the earth at the same rate as the sun—once a year instead of once a month—this would not keep the high tide in being. We are no doubt expected to recognize this; Aurelius's delirium is to be seen in the irrationality of what he prays for, not in the manner of his speech, and indeed this irrationality will only be apparent if lucidly expounded.

Aurelius keeps up his elaborate prayer for 49 lines, and then immediately swoons,

> And longe time he lay forth in a traunce.   (409)

We now get a further description of his misery, still in terms of the courtly convention. According to this convention, passionate love is literally to be thought of as a disease. This disease is referred to in *The Knight's Tale* as 'Hereos, the loveris maladye', and its symptoms are those of a prolonged bout of influenza. Aurelius takes to his bed, and for 'two yeer and moore' (430) is unable to walk. He tells no one but his brother of the cause of his illness, and his brother sees that he must be *warisshed* (cured) (466). The only cure is for him to obtain Dorigen's love, and so the magician is brought in. Henceforward the characterization of Aurelius becomes less conventional, and we shall return to it shortly.

The Garden

The conventional characterization of *The Franklin's Tale* will naturally be set in an equally conventional scenic background. We have seen that in many respects the topography of the Tale is detailed and realistic, and the black rocks, in particular, are a real geographical feature which does not belong to any literary convention. There is, however, another kind of scenery in the poem, which is exemplified most fully, with striking dramatic contrast, immediately after the speech in which Dorigen asks for what purpose the rocks were created. She is persuaded by her friends to give up her brooding watch on the coast and to join them on a picnic in a garden. We follow them there, and we are told that the season is May. The springtime garden which is now described is typical and general rather than specific, and belongs to a widespread convention in medieval literature which is also found in the garden descriptions of *The Knight's Tale* and *The Merchant's Tale*. Its origins are to be found in the pastoral literature of antiquity, and also in the descriptions of the garden of Eden in *Genesis* and of the heavenly Jerusalem in *Revelation*. Under the influence particularly of the *Roman de la Rose*, a thirteenth-century French poem which Chaucer had himself translated into English, this Maytime garden had become the traditional setting for love adventures. The description of it, like that of Aurelius, who is linked with it by the May comparison, is symbolic rather than realistic, though no doubt real medieval gardens also followed the pattern of the literary convention. The landscape does not so much exist of itself, like the irremovable black rocks, as in order to embody a specific set of feelings connected with love. The garden of love in the first part of the *Roman de la Rose*, written by Guillaume de Lorris, was described as a kind of paradise, and was inhabited by a god, Cupid, the god of love; but in the continuation written some forty years later by Jean de Meun a contrast was drawn between this secular pseudo-paradise and the true paradise of the Christian religion. In *The Franklin's Tale* description this contrast is hinted at:

> That nevere was ther gardyn of swich prys,
> But if it were the verray paradis.   (239–40)

The garden is less paradisal than it seems; it is indeed all too like the garden of Eden, for it contains a serpent, in the person of Aurelius. A garden scene had been used with exactly similar ambiguity by the Merchant in his Tale, where a young squire had used it to seduce a married woman in her husband's very presence. This time, however, the wife resists temptation, and an echo of the Fall is avoided.

REALISM

Much of the framework of *The Franklin's Tale*, then, is supplied by the conventions of courtly literature. To some extent, no doubt, courtly life followed these conventions too—just as, in the twentieth century, there has been influence in both directions between the way people conduct love-affairs in real life and the way they have been presented on the cinema screen. But in general these conventions, though they can have a positive value of their own, do not represent in any detail the way people actually behave and speak. If the whole of *The Franklin's Tale* had been like this, it would have been a work as remote and pageant-like as *The Knight's Tale*. The impressions the two works make on us are very different, though; and a large part of the difference is accounted for by the presence of many touches of realism throughout *The Franklin's Tale*, which make the characters stop being merely dancers in a courtly dance, and start behaving like real people. The action will have been following an established courtly pattern for some time, and then a particular scene will seize the narrator's imagination, and will be realized dramatically as a new and unpredictable human experience. We shall see this happening very clearly if we turn back for a moment to Aurelius, whom we have seen so fully presented in terms of the conventions of courtly love. In all the swooning and sickness and singing of 'layes, Songes, compleintes, roundels, virelayes' there has been one striking human touch to add conviction to the traditional account of the lover's sufferings. It is presented as an exception: he dares disclose nothing of his love to Dorigen,

> Save that, paraventure, somtime at daunces,
> Ther yonge folk kepen hir observaunces,
> It may wel be he looked on hir face
> In swich a wise as man that asketh grace;
> But nothing wiste she of his entente.   (283–7)

This mute look, lost in the noise and bustle of the dance, and not understood, presented by the narrator with a hesitance (*It may wel be . . .*) that echoes Aurelius's own, brings the whole convention to life. When Aurelius finally does pluck up courage to declare himself to Dorigen, he does so in a speech which belongs entirely to the convention, full of the jargon of service, pity, pain, and death, and rhetorically organized with great lucidity. Dorigen's reaction is of another kind altogether, unpredictable and lifelike:

> She gan to looke upon Aurelius:
> 'Is this youre wil,' quod she, 'and sey ye thus?
> Nevere erst,' quod she, 'ne wiste I what ye mente'.   (307–9)

Her innocent incredulity is utterly convincing. First there is a pause as she stares at him, taking in the force of what he has said, and seeming to see him for the first time (for all her thoughts have been devoted to her absent husband). Then she almost stammers out her reply, the stammer being suggested by the way *quod she* twice interrupts her answer in mid-sentence. She goes on to give a downright refusal, but immediately qualifies it with a condition that only re-emphasizes her rejection of his advances. She will become his mistress after all—*if* he can remove all the rocks from the coast of Brittany. Still the scene is realized in human terms. He answers, taking her condition seriously, with white-faced desperation:

> 'Is ther noon oother grace in yow?' quod he.   (327)

Her reply is once again downright and unashamedly innocent, in its blunt question that strikes at the whole root of the courtly convention:

> 'No, by that Lord,' quod she, 'that maked me.
> For wel I woot that it shal never bitide.
> Lat swiche folies out of youre herte slide.
> What deyntee sholde a man han in his lyf
> For to go love another mannes wyf,
> That hath hir body whan so that him liketh?'   (328–33)

43

He turns away with a melodramatic threat of death, and immediately her other friends appear, knowing nothing of the dramatic little scene that has just been played out, and ready to begin some new entertainment. The whole episode has been created with burning vividness, and we have been brought for a moment to experience it through the consciousnesses of the characters themselves, as they first become aware of each other's true natures.

A second point in the poem where the conventional is touched with the realistic is the part dealing with the consequences of the magician's success in causing the rocks to vanish. Aurelius first thanks the magician and, in the same sentence, Venus, and then goes to a temple where he expects to find Dorigen, and tells her what has happened. The speech in which he does so (639–66) begins as a formal *pleynt*, like his earlier prayer to Apollo, and with a similarly composed and logical syntax, which seems to belie his emotion:

> 'My righte lady,' quod this woful man,
> 'Whom I moost drede and love as I best kan,
> And lothest were of al this world displese,
> Nere it that I for yow have swich disese
> That I moste dien heere at youre foot anon,
> Noght wolde I telle how me is wo bigon'. (639–44)

Once more he is using the conventional jargon of *fine amour*, and it seems that the main point is being evaded. It soon becomes clear that this evasion is deliberate. Aurelius is at once embarrassed and wildly excited; he is unable to bring himself to the point, and is using the convention as a barrier against his own emotion. Gradually, however, the emotion breaks through the lucid rhetorical structure, and he loses himself in parentheses that are intended to be reassuring but are in fact merely confusing:

> For, madame, wel ye woot what ye han hight—
> Nat that I chalange any thing of right
> Of yow, my soverein lady, but youre grace—
> But in a gardyn yond, at swich a place,
> Ye woot right wel what ye bihighten me... (651–5)

He cannot bring himself to say directly either what she promised or what he has done, and it is not till the last line of the whole speech that he first mentions the crucial word *rokkes*. This speech

44

exemplifies perfectly the Chaucerian blend of convention and realism. The convention is as necessary as its opposite, for it has to exist in order to be so convincingly broken down.

Dorigen's immediate reaction to Aurelius's disclosure is a stunned silence which is all the more convincing after his diffuseness:

> He taketh his leve, and she astoned stood;
> In al hir face nas a drope of blood.
> She wende nevere han come in swich a trappe. (667–9)

The bluntness of the word *trappe* is more powerful than any rhetoric; but only because it is surrounded by passages in a rhetorical 'high style'. Once she has collected herself, she shows the conventional signs of grief—

> She wepeth, wailleth, al a day or two,
> And swowneth, that it routhe was to see (676–7)

—and then embarks on the immensely long lament which we have already considered at an earlier stage of this Introduction as a rhetorical set-piece. It begins with an *exclamatio* directed against Fortune (a figure who is regularly invoked to account for unhappy situations in medieval poetry), and then goes on to list twenty-two *exempla* of women who died rather than face the dishonour that faces her. I have suggested that the excessive length of this list is partly intended as a piece of ostentation on the Franklin's part, and thus as a joke against him shared by Chaucer and his more judicious readers. It also has its part to play in the realism of the poem, unlikely as that may seem. The point of it, so far as our understanding of Dorigen is concerned, surely lies in the contrast between its ostensible purpose and what follows from it. Dorigen uses the *exempla* to prove conclusively to herself that the only way out of her dilemma is suicide, but in the end, after

> a day or tweye,
> Purposinge evere that she wolde deye, (785–6)

she does not die at all, but simply confesses to her husband, and leaves it to him to decide what she ought to do. In the course of the speech we can watch her struggling to take the heroic resolution which she believes to be the right one, but struggling in vain. She begins with an *exemplum* laden with expressions of exaggerated horror—'ful of cursednesse...in despit...God yeve

45

hem meschaunce!'—and culminating in the wonderfully implausible picture of a number of virgins jumping *secretly* into a well to drown themselves. It has a fine ripe flavour of absurdity which should prepare us for what is to come. The succeeding *exempla*, growing shorter and less to the point as her desperation increases, serve not as a way of nerving herself to act, but as a way of delaying till her husband comes home and can tell her what to do. They include references to one lady who killed herself not through fear of dishonour but through anxiety about her husband during his absence (a situation closer to Dorigen's than she realizes), and one about a lady who built her husband a splendid tomb after his death (a situation so spectacularly irrelevant as to indicate approaching hysteria). The list concludes with a couplet mentioning three names chosen with a total disregard for relevance, being those of a lady who refused to marry a second time, a second who killed her nurse for trying to persuade her to marry a second time, and a third who showed her *parfit wyfhod* by putting up with her husband's bad breath. At this point Arveragus returns, and she pours the whole story out to him. Dorigen falls short of the heroic, and the effect is of bathos. This is Chaucer's point in the speech, though for the Franklin, if we have him in mind at this moment, no doubt the speech is entirely serious, and grandly shows how Dorigen laments 'as doon thise noble wives whan hem liketh' (146). The scene which follows on her husband's arrival is also treated with human realism. It is a scene we have returned to more than once already, but it may be worth glancing again at its early stages:

> Hoom cam Arveragus, this worthy knight,
> And asked hire why that she weep so soore;
> And she gan wepen ever lenger the moore.
> 'Allas,' quod she, 'that evere was I born!
> Thus have I seyd,' quod she, 'thus have I sworn'—
> And toold him al as ye han herd bifore.   (788–93)

It seems very natural that his question should cause redoubled weeping, and, when she does at last manage to answer, repeated *quod she*'s are again used deliberately to imitate the interruption of her speech, this time by sobs. And now, after the rhetorical profusion of her lament, there follows a brief scene of intense human interest, in which emotion is restrained yet implied by terseness of speech, and at last finds issue in tears, this time shed by Arveragus.

Introduction

We have been studying the realism of *The Franklin's Tale* in two fairly extended sequences of the poem, but it is also to be found in small touches scattered almost at random over the conventional framework. Here I may mention two of them. Dorigen's friends try to comfort her sorrow at her husband's absence by arranging a dance in the garden after dinner, but this device has the opposite effect to what they intend. She was even more miserable,

> For she ne saugh him on the daunce go
> That was hir housbonde and hir love also.   (249–50)

The slight unexpectedness of this is lifelike and touching. And when the Clerk has promised Aurelius that for a thousand pounds he will make the rocks vanish, we are told that at last Aurelius got a good night's sleep, after his two years of misery and insomnia:

> To bedde is goon Aurelius whan him leste,
> And wel ny al that night he hadde his reste.
> What for his labour and his hope of blisse,
> His woful herte of penaunce hadde a lisse.   (563–6)

It is not only his hope of achieving his desire but also his hard work in rushing to Orleans and persuading the Clerk to do what he wishes that sends him to sleep. The detail is not strictly necessary, but it makes us believe for a moment in the two years of conventional love-sickness. There are many other such touches of realism in the poem, which the reader will discover for himself.

The Black Rocks

We have considered the kind of symbolism in the poem that belongs to its conventional framework, in the example of the garden. *The Franklin's Tale* also contains a somewhat different kind of symbolism which is the product of its human realism, a symbolism that is developed under the pressure of human emotions, and that sometimes changes its meaning startlingly as the human situation changes. The most striking example of this non-conventional symbolism in the poem is that of the black rocks round the coast of Brittany. We have seen that these rocks are a real geographical feature, belonging to that detailed Breton topography that forms one part of the poem's realism. The significance of the

47

rocks, though, lies not in their mere genuineness, but in the imaginative force they acquire from the play of Dorigen's emotions on them. They are transformed into symbols by Dorigen herself, and we must begin by examining the great speech (193–221) in which she asks for what purpose they have been created. After her husband has left 'To seke in armes worship and honour' (139) in England, she walks on the sea-shore at her friends' persuasion 'hire to disporte' (177). But first she regrets that none of the ships she sees is bringing her husband home to her, and then her attention turns to 'the grisly rokkes blake' round the coast, and these fill her with fear. Her thoughts and feelings are represented in a speech arraigning the divine ordering of the universe, which is perhaps the most urgent and deeply felt passage in the whole poem. Its basic material is philosophical, and is borrowed in part from a favourite philosophical work of Chaucer's, the *De Consolatione Philosophiae* of Boethius, which he had himself translated from Latin into English. Much of its phrasing recalls Chaucer's translation, and in particular the speech in which Boethius himself, in his dialogue with Philosophy, asks why God, who orders the whole non-human world with such regularity, leaves human life to the disorderly and arbitrary government of Fortune. In the *De Consolatione*, however, there are no black rocks to form an anomaly in the non-human world as well. It is they that form the imaginative centre of Dorigen's speech, a concrete instance to challenge the generalizations of philosophy. The philosophical content of the speech is marshalled into the form of an argument addressed to God—one side of an imaginary disputation, in which the other party remains silent—but it is also presented, somewhat similarly to the speech in which Aurelius announces to Dorigen that the miracle has been performed, in such a way as to express intense feeling. The bland confidence and ordered rhetorical high style of her first sentence—

> Eterne God, that thurgh thy purveiaunce
> Ledest the world by certein governaunce,
> In idel, as men seyn, ye no thing make

—is interrupted by the eager familiarity of her second, where the rocks themselves, surrounded by a spurt of emotive epithets, elbow aside the normal syntactical structure, so that the first four lines of the sentence are in apposition to the object of a verb for which room cannot be found until the fifth line:

> But, Lord, thise grisly feendly rokkes blake,
> That semen rather a foul confusion
> Of werk than any fair creacion
> Of swich a parfit wys God and a stable,
> Why han ye wroght this werk unresonable?

Notice also the emphasis given to *why* by the delay. Dorigen, full of the horror aroused by seeing the rocks, abruptly takes God to task, and cannot leave him alone, though at one point she turns aside to conduct a brief contemptuous argument with the scholars who would defend him:

> I woot wel clerkes wol seyn as hem leste,
> By argumentz, that al is for the beste,
> Though I ne kan the causes nat yknowe.
> But thilke God that made wind to blowe
> As kepe my Lord! this my conclusion.
> To clerkes lete I al disputison.

Again and again she reverts to the rocks themselves, the one horrifyingly undeniable fact in an utterly dubious metaphysical situation.

This speech is similar in many ways to one in *The Knight's Tale*, in which Palamon asks what the gods care for men. In both cases, arguments borrowed from the *De Consolatione*, and there used *against* Philosophy, are presented with passionate conviction and concrete illustration, while Philosophy's answers are omitted. In *The Knight's Tale* it is the pagan gods who are assumed to be the rulers of the universe, and whom Palamon arraigns, but in *The Franklin's Tale*, though the setting is again pagan, there is no indication in this particular speech that anyone but the Christian God is being considered. The God addressed by Dorigen is a perfect, eternal, and immutable creator, who has made man in his own image (as in *Genesis*), and whose ways are justified by *clerkes*. And Dorigen uses throughout the language of medieval Christian scholasticism—*purveiaunce, argumentz, causes, conclusion, disputison*. The speech is moving and disturbing, and it cannot be said, I think, either that it is answered at a later stage of the poem or that it can be brought within the cloak of Christian orthodoxy. It does not necessarily represent Chaucer's own considered view of the universe, of course, any more than Macbeth's 'Tomorrow, and tomorrow, and tomorrow' speech represents Shakespeare's. But, as in the case of

Macbeth, there can be no doubt that Dorigen's situation and her questionings have engaged the poet's feelings and imagination at a very deep level; he has for the moment *become* Dorigen.

In this speech of Dorigen's, the black rocks, under the influence of her own *derke fantasye* (172), have become a symbol of some flaw in the divinely ordered course of nature. But her feelings change, and as they do so, the symbolism of the rocks changes too. The rocks are constantly in her mind, as potential dangers to her husband, and it is for this reason, no doubt, that when Aurelius declares his love for her she answers that she will love him in return if

> ...endelong Britaine
> Ye remoeve alle the rokkes, stoon by stoon,
> That they ne lette ship ne boot to goon.   (320–2)

Reverting to the role of courtly mistress, she sets her lover an apparently impossible task to perform as the condition of obtaining her love, but the very nature of the task she thinks of shows that what is closest to her heart is still her husband and his safety, not her lover. Moreover, she does not believe the task to be possible—'wel I woot that it shal never bitide' (329)—and so the rocks, from being an irrational anomaly in the ordering of the world, now come to be a sign of the immutable natural order itself. Aurelius goes away, and Dorigen presumably thinks no more of the matter. At length he returns, long after Arveragus has come safely back to her, with the news that the task has been performed. Her reaction confirms that the symbolism of the rocks has completely reversed its significance, and they now stand for a stable natural order which can be overturned only by some monstrous illusion:

> 'Allas,' quod she, 'that evere this sholde happe!
> For wende I nevere by possibilitee
> That swich a monstre or merveille mighte be!
> It is agains the proces of nature.'   (670–3)

Magic

Discussion of the black rocks and their symbolic significance leads us naturally into a consideration of the nature of the magic by which they are made to vanish. If they are ambiguous, so ought the magic to be, and so indeed we shall find it. From its first introduction, the magic of *The Franklin's Tale* is treated in a way which can fairly be called 'realistic'. It may seem absurd to us to treat such a subject with realism, but in the Middle Ages it was not so, for magic and science were by no means completely separated. There was thus a real distinction between treating magic fantastically, as it is treated in the Breton lays, or in *Sir Gawain and the Green Knight*, and treating it realistically. In *Sir Gawain and the Green Knight*, it is by magic that Sir Bertilak de Hautdesert has been given his second identity as the Green Knight, and this magic is treated at once fantastically (to thrill and mystify us) and conventionally (to provide the basic machinery of the story); but the author shows no interest in the actual magical processes by which the marvel has been carried out. In *The Franklin's Tale*, on the other hand, even though the ultimate details are left vague, our attention is very much focused on the magical process itself, and it is treated as a scientific process. When the possibility of magic is first suggested, by Aurelius's brother when he is trying to think how Aurelius can be cured, it is a book of *magik natureel* that he remembers seeing left by a friend on a desk at Orleans. Natural magic was firmly distinguished in the Middle Ages from black magic; it was considered legitimate by many theological authorities, and it was thought of as a form of science, which made use not of spirits but of a special knowledge of natural phenomena. The natural phenomena concerned in the book he saw and throughout the poem are planetary influences, and there was nothing diabolic or illusory about these for the Middle Ages. It was generally believed that the seven 'planets' (including the sun and the moon) which were then known influenced human life and earthly events generally, and influenced them in various ways according to the positions of the planets in the heavens and in relation to each other. In the particular case involved in the story, magic and science were indeed very close, for the moon and sun really do influence the tides, and could thus be responsible for covering up the rocks. This is what Aurelius prays for to Apollo, the sun-god, but prayer is not enough, and natural magic has to be resorted to. Already, though, the Franklin himself is taking up a definite attitude against all magic, natural or otherwise:

> Which book spak muchel of the operaciouns
> Touchinge the eighte and twenty mansiouns
> That longen to the moone, and swich folye

As in oure dayes is nat worth a flye;
For hooly chirches feith in oure bileve
Ne suffreth noon illusioun us to greve.   (457–62)

A double attitude towards magic is thus present from this very
first speech in which it is mentioned. It is at once *natureel* and
illusioun. This double attitude can be felt as the Franklin's own
—he is at once fascinated by magic and determined to take the
side of extreme respectability against it—but it also acts as a
reflexion on the desire which the magic is intended to fulfil.
Whatever the means used, however scientific the experiment,
Aurelius's hope of achieving Dorigen's love is itself illusory.
Hence the double emphasis throughout, on the elaborately
scientific nature of the Clerk's experiment, and on the fact that
its result is only *illusioun* or *apparence*:

For with an apparence a clerk may make,
To mannes sighte, that alle the rokkes blake
Of Britaigne weren yvoided everichon.   (485–7)

But it is only *to mannes sighte*, and the word *seme* is used again
and again to remind us of the illusion involved. What Aurelius
aims at is an illusion, an escape from reality, and only by an
illusion can he attempt to achieve it.

The ambiguous nature of magic in the poem is especially
apparent in the series of feats that the Clerk performs for
Aurelius on his arrival in his house:

He shewed him, er he wente to sopeer,
Forestes, parkes ful of wilde deer;
Ther saugh he hertes with hir hornes hye,
The gretteste that evere were seyn with ye.
He saugh of hem an hondred slain with houndes,
And somme with arwes blede of bittre woundes.
He saugh, whan voided were thise wilde deer,
Thise fauconers upon a fair river,
That with hir haukes han the heron slain.
Tho saugh he knightes justing in a plain;
And after this he dide him swich plesaunce
That he him shewed his lady on a daunce,
On which himself he daunced, as him thoughte.
     (517–29)

52

The practical purpose of this demonstration is to act as bait, to encourage Aurelius to hire the Clerk's services. The scenes shown, therefore, as Professor Hodgson has put it in her edition of the Tale, are 'shrewdly selected to appeal to a young squire, whose own pastimes are hunting, hawking, jousting, and dancing'. But from another point of view the same scenes are a series of visions of death and destruction, culminating in the illusion of himself dancing with Dorigen. Thus the dead and bleeding harts, the dead heron, and the jousting knights together form an implicit comment on the nature of Aurelius's passion: it too is destructive, an urge towards death (as his long illness shows in more conventional terms), not towards life. The vision of the harts is particularly effective, for they are bleeding with *bittre woundes* from arrows, and the metaphor of love as a death-dealing arrow has been applied only recently to Aurelius himself:

> But in his herte ay was the arwe kene. (440)

It is at least possible that the connexion is made even closer by a pun on his *herte* and the dying *hertes* of the vision. This pun almost certainly occurs in Chaucer's early poem *The Book of the Duchess*, and it may well be present here too. Whether it is or not, the sudden disappearance of the last vision, in which Aurelius dances with Dorigen, comments further on the illusory nature of his passion, as well as luring him further into the Clerk's power.

The final appearance of magic in the Tale is in the description of the actual experiment by which the Clerk makes the rocks vanish. He waits for a suitable opportunity (591), because the position of the planets is vitally important, and he chooses correctly, according to the science of astrology, early January, when the moon is in a particularly powerful position. The Franklin again casts scorn on the science used—

> So atte laste he hath his time yfounde
> To maken his japes and his wrecchednesse
> Of swich a supersticious cursednesse (598–600)

—and contrasts this illusory practice of heathen times with Christian truth—

> And knew also his othere observaunces
> For swiche illusiouns and swiche meschaunces
> As hethen folk useden in thilke dayes. (619–21)

Nevertheless he once more shows his fascination with astrology, in an ostentatious display of its technical jargon. The ambiguity of magic remains to the very end, the last two lines of the description being:

> ...thurgh his magik, for a wyke or tweye,
> It semed that alle the rokkes were aweye.   (623–4)

The statement that *the rokkes were aweye* comes emphatically as the climax to a long description, but it is still preceded by *it semed*. There is no way, of course, of resolving the ambiguity. There is no way of deciding whether the Clerk's magic was 'really' *natureel* or *illusioun*, for we know only what we are told about it in the Tale. Its ambiguity is essential and intentional, for it must at once produce the effect of removing the rocks and indicate that Aurelius, in having this miracle performed, is still only pursuing an illusion.

CONCLUSION

Our account of *The Franklin's Tale* has found it to be full of doubts and ambiguities. The Tale ends with a question—which was the most generous of the three men?—to which no answer is given by the Franklin, and which he leaves it to the other pilgrims to settle. It would be a mistake to assume either that this question is merely conventional or that it has a 'right' answer. Medieval courtly poems do tend to conclude with a *demande*, but this convention is genuinely functional. In medieval society, poetry was a pastime, a form of communal entertainment, and if a poem provided matter for discussion after it was ended, so much the better, for conversation was another favourite form of entertainment. *The Franklin's Tale* does indeed provide much matter for discussion; not only the question of *franchise*, but also those of *gentillesse* more generally, of *trouthe*, of the place of *maistrie* in marriage, of the reliability of magic, and perhaps others. On all these topics, the Tale offers evidence on more than one side; it incites its audience (whether we think of this as being the Franklin's audience of pilgrims or Chaucer's own audience) to make their own judgements, but it does not tell them what judgements they are to make. A central image in the Tale is the double-bearded Janus, and he might be taken to stand for the Franklin, offering a double perspective on the convincingly human world of his Tale.

Introduction

Are we to conclude, then, that the total effect of *The Franklin's Tale* is problematic? A comparison with Shakespeare will make clear what is meant. A number of Shakespeare's plays have come in this century to be called 'problem plays', or sometimes tragicomedies; among them are usually included *Measure for Measure* and *All's Well That Ends Well*. In both these plays central characters seem to fit only with difficulty into the roles that romantic stories have ordained for them, and one at least in each play—the Duke in *Measure for Measure* and Helena in *All's Well*—seems to exist partly on a human and partly on a supernatural plane of being. As a result, the very titles of the plays seem to invite questioning: *has* measure been dealt out for measure? and *is* all made well by ending well? These plays do not merely raise separate problems of interpretation, but present a whole view of life which is itself problematic. Is *The Franklin's Tale*, with all its unresolved ambiguities, a work of this kind, which we ought to refer to as 'a problem poem'?

The answer to this question is, I think, 'no', and to be able to say this is to go some way towards defining the nature of *The Franklin's Tale*. There is an urgency in Shakespeare's problem plays that involves us deeply in their questionings, and their questionings do not merely interest or intrigue, they disturb. On the whole this urgency pressing us towards a radical disquiet is not to be found in *The Franklin's Tale*, except at one point. That point is Dorigen's speech in which she questions the divine ordering of the universe; a speech which, moving though it is, is a loose end in the poem, asking questions which are not merely unanswered but completely dropped. The contrast between Divine providence and the state of the world was a subject by which Chaucer's imagination was easily stirred, and which he treats in others of his poems with an urgency too great to be fitted into the overall scheme of the work. Apart from this speech, however, Chaucer seems to be careful to keep his work below the level of the disturbingly problematic. It is not that he is unable to reach this level, but that he is aiming at something different. Again and again, when there is a particular danger that we shall become too deeply engaged in the suffering of his characters and the issues that it might raise, he finds some means of drawing us back, reminding us that it is only a tale told by a Franklin, or that the eventual outcome will be happy for everyone. Thus, near the beginning, when Dorigen is left alone by

55

her husband and falls into acute misery, we are warned by a word of patronizing admiration from the Franklin for the nobility of her grief not to take it too seriously:

> For his absence wepeth she and siketh,
> As doon thise noble wives whan hem liketh.   (145–6)

When Aurelius falls into a similarly despairing state, and has to be put to bed by his brother, the Franklin again draws us back from too deep a sympathy with a callous transitional comment:

> Dispeyred in this torment and this thoght
> Lete I this woful creature lie;
> Chese he, for me, wheither he wol live or die.
>
> (412–14)

Dorigen's lament is a large-scale example of how to blunt the cutting-edge of grief by allowing it to become slightly absurd. And, towards the end, when Arveragus seems to be confronted by his wife's confession with as painful and disturbing a dilemma as the choice Isabella has to make in *Measure for Measure* between her brother and her chastity, we are twice given the hint that the outcome will be happy after all. First Arveragus himself expresses a vague hope, in the course of cheering Dorigen up—

> It may be wel, paraventure, yet to day   (801)

—and then the Franklin himself intervenes, to warn us not to be too hasty in our responses:

> Paraventure an heep of yow, ywis,
> Wol holden him a lewed man in this
> That he wol putte his wyf in jupartie.
> Herkneth the tale er ye upon hire crie.
> She may have bettre fortune than yow semeth;
> And whan that ye han herd the tale, demeth.
>
> (821–6)

Judgement is to be reserved till we have heard the whole tale; Chaucer's aim is not to press us into judgement by the urgency of separate situations, but to intrigue and interest us until the complete story provides material for endless discussion. In this aim he has admirably succeeded.

NOTE ON THE TEXT

The text which follows is based upon that of F. N. Robinson (*The Complete Works of Geoffrey Chaucer*, 2nd ed., 1957). The punctuation has been revised, with special reference to the exclamation marks. Spelling has been partly rationalized, by substituting *i* for *y* wherever the change aids the modern reader and does not affect the semantic value of the word. Thus *smylyng* becomes 'smiling', and *nyghtyngale* 'nightingale', but *wyn* (wine), *lyk* (like), and *fyr* (fire) are allowed to stand.

No accentuation has been provided in this text, for two reasons. First, because it produces a page displeasing to the eye; secondly, because it no longer seems necessary or entirely reliable in the light of modern scholarship. It is not now thought that the later works of Chaucer were written in a ten-syllable line from which no variation was permissible. The correct reading of a line of Chaucer is now seen to be more closely related to the correct reading of a comparable line of prose with phrasing suited to the rhythms of speech. This allows the reader to be more flexible in his interpretation of the line, and makes it unreasonably pedantic to provide a rigid system of accentuation.

NOTE ON PRONUNCIATION

These equivalences are intended to offer only a rough guide. For further detail, see *An Introduction to Chaucer*.

SHORT VOWELS

ă represents the sound now written *u*, as in 'cut'

ĕ as in modern 'set'

ĭ as in modern 'is'

ŏ as in modern 'top'

ŭ as in modern 'put' (not as in 'cut')

final -*e* represents the neutral vowel sound in '*a*bout' or 'atten*tio*n'. It is silent when the next word in the line begins with a vowel or an *h*

Note on the Text

LONG VOWELS

ā as in modern 'car' (not as in 'name')

ē (open—i.e. where the equivalent modern word is spelt with *ea*) as in modern 'there'

ē (close—i.e. where the equivalent modern word is spelt with *ee* or *e*) represents the sound now written *a* as in 'take'

ī as in modern 'machine' (not as in 'like')

ō (open—i.e. where the equivalent modern vowel is pronounced as in 'brother', 'mood', or 'good') represents the sound now written *aw* as in 'fawn'

ō (close—i.e. where the equivalent modern vowel is pronounced as in 'road') as in modern 'note'

ū as in French *tu* or German *Tür*

DIPHTHONGS

ai and *ei* both roughly represent the sound now written *i* or *y* as in 'die' or 'dye'

au and *aw* both represent the sound now written *ow* or *ou* as in 'now' or 'pounce'

ou and *ow* have two pronunciations: as in *through* where the equivalent modern vowel is pronounced as in 'through' or 'mouse'; and as in *pounce* where the equivalent modern vowel is pronounced as in 'know' or 'thought'

WRITING OF VOWELS AND DIPHTHONGS

A long vowel is often indicated by doubling, as in *roote* or *eek*. The *ŭ* sound is sometimes represented by an *o* as in *yong*. The *au* sound is sometimes represented by an *a*, especially before *m* or *n*, as in *cha(u)mbre* or *cha(u)nce*.

CONSONANTS

Largely as in modern English, except that many consonants now silent were still pronounced. *Gh* was pronounced as in Scottish 'lo*ch*', and both consonants should be pronounced in such groups as the following: '*gn*acchen', '*kn*ave', 'wo*rd*', 'fo*lk*', '*wr*ong'.

THE FRANKLIN'S PROLOGUE

Heere folwen the wordes of the Frankeleyn to the
Squier, and the wordes of the Hoost to the Frankeleyn.

'In feith, Squier, thow hast thee wel yquit
And gentilly. I preise wel thy wit,'
Quod the Frankeleyn, 'consideringe thy yowthe,
So feelingly thou spekest, sire, I allow the.
As to my doom, ther is noon that is heere
Of eloquence that shal be thy peere,
If that thou live; God yeve thee good chaunce,
And in vertu sende thee continuaunce!
For of thy speche I have greet deyntee.
I have a sone, and by the Trinitee,   10
I hadde levere than twenty pound worth lond,
Though it right now were fallen in myn hond,
He were a man of swich discrecioun
As that ye been. Fy on possessioun,
But if a man be vertuous withal!
I have my sone snybbed, and yet shal,
For he to vertu listeth nat entende;
But for to pleye at dees, and to despende
And lese al that he hath, is his usage.
And he hath levere talken with a page   20
Than to comune with any gentil wight
Where he mighte lerne gentillesse aright.'
'Straw for youre gentillesse!' quod oure Hoost.
'What, Frankeleyn! pardee, sire, wel thou woost
That ech of yow moot tellen atte leste
A tale or two, or breken his biheste.'
'That knowe I wel, sire,' quod the Frankeleyn.

'I prey yow, haveth me nat in desdeyn,
Though to this man I speke a word or two.'
30   'Telle on thy tale withouten wordes mo.'
'Gladly, sire Hoost,' quod he, 'I wole obeye
Unto your wil; now herkneth what I seye.
I wol yow nat contrarien in no wise
As fer as that my wittes wol suffise.
I prey to God that it may plesen yow;
Thanne woot I wel that it is good ynow.'

The Prologe of the Frankeleyns Tale

Thise olde gentil Britouns in hir dayes
Of diverse aventures maden layes,
Rimeyed in hir firste Briton tonge;
40   Whiche layes with hir instrumentz they songe,
Or elles redden hem for hir plesaunce,
And oon of hem have I in remembraunce,
Which I shal seyn with good wil as I kan.
But sires, by cause I am a burel man,
At my biginning first I yow biseche,
Have me excused of my rude speche.
I lerned nevere rethorik, certeyn;
Thing that I speke, it moot be bare and pleyn.
I sleep nevere on the Mount of Pernaso,
50   Ne lerned Marcus Tullius Scithero.
Colours ne knowe I none, withouten drede,
But swiche colours as growen in the mede,
Or elles swiche as men dye or peynte.
Colours of rethorik been to me queynte;
My spirit feeleth noght of swich mateere.
But if yow list, my tale shul ye heere.

THE FRANKLIN'S TALE

In Armorik, that called is Britaine,
Ther was a knight that loved and dide his paine
To serve a lady in his beste wise;
And many a labour, many a greet emprise   60
He for his lady wroghte, er she were wonne.
For she was oon the faireste under sonne,
And eek therto comen of so heigh kinrede
That wel unnethes dorste this knight, for drede,
Telle hire his wo, his peyne, and his distresse.
But atte laste she, for his worthinesse,
And namely for his meke obeisaunce,
Hath swich a pitee caught of his penaunce
That prively she fil of his accord
To take him for hir housbonde and hir lord,   70
Of swich lordshipe as men han over hir wives.
And for to lede the moore in blisse hir lives,
Of his free wil he swoor hire as a knight
That nevere in al his lyf he, day ne night,
Ne sholde upon him take no maistrie
Again hir wil, ne kithe hire jalousie,
But hire obeye, and folwe hir wil in al,
As any lovere to his lady shal,
Save that the name of soverainetee,
That wolde he have for shame of his degree.   80
    She thanked him, and with ful greet humblesse
She seyde, 'Sire, sith of youre gentillesse
Ye profre me to have so large a reine,
Ne wolde nevere God bitwixe us tweyne,
As in my gilt, were outher werre or stryf.

Sire, I wol be youre humble trewe wyf,
Have heer my trouthe, til that myn herte breste.'
Thus been they bothe in quiete and in reste.

    For o thing, sires, saufly dar I seye,
90   That freendes everich oother moot obeye,
If they wol longe holden compaignye.
Love wol nat been constreyned by maistrye.
Whan maistrie comth, the God of Love anon
Beteth his winges, and farewel, he is gon!
Love is a thing as any spirit free.
Wommen, of kinde, desiren libertee,
And nat to been constreyned as a thral;
And so doon men, if I sooth seyen shal.
Looke who that is moost pacient in love,
100   He is at his avantage al above.
Pacience is an heigh vertu, certeyn,
For it venquisseth, as thise clerkes seyn,
Thinges that rigour sholde nevere atteyne.
For every word men may nat chide or pleyne.
Lerneth to suffre, or elles, so moot I goon,
Ye shul it lerne, wher so ye wole or noon;
For in this world, certein, ther no wight is
That he ne dooth or seith somtime amis.
Ire, siknesse, or constellacioun,
110   Wyn, wo, or chauonginge of complexioun
Causeth ful ofte to doon amis or speken.
On every wrong a man may nat be wreken.
After the time moste be temperaunce
To every wight that kan on governaunce.
And therfore hath this wise, worthy knight,
To live in ese, suffrance hire bihight,
And she to him ful wisly gan to swere

That nevere sholde ther be defaute in here.
  Heere may men seen an humble, wys accord;
Thus hath she take hir servant and hir lord—   120
Servant in love, and lord in mariage.
Thanne was he bothe in lordshipe and servage.
Servage? nay, but in lordshipe above,
Sith he hath bothe his lady and his love;
His lady, certes, and his wyf also,
The which that lawe of love acordeth to.
And whan he was in this prosperitee,
Hoom with his wyf he gooth to his contree,
Nat fer fro Pedmark, ther his dwelling was,
Where as he liveth in blisse and in solas.   130
  Who koude telle, but he hadde wedded be,
The joye, the ese, and the prosperitee
That is bitwixe an housbonde and his wyf?
A yeer and moore lasted this blisful lyf,
Til that the knight of which I speke of thus,
That of Kayrrud was cleped Arveragus,
Shoop him to goon and dwelle a yeer or tweyne
In Engelond, that cleped was eek Briteyne,
To seke in armes worshipe and honour;
For al his lust he sette in swich labour;   140
And dwelled there two yeer, the book seith thus.
  Now wol I stynten of this Arveragus,
And speken I wole of Dorigen his wyf,
That loveth hire housbonde as hire hertes lyf.
For his absence wepeth she and siketh,
As doon thise noble wives whan hem liketh.
She moorneth, waketh, waileth, fasteth, pleyneth;
Desir of his presence hire so destreyneth
That al this wide world she sette at noght.

150   Hire freendes, whiche that knewe hir hevy thoght,
Conforten hire in al that ever they may.
They prechen hire, they telle hire night and day
That causelees she sleeth hirself, allas!
And every confort possible in this cas
They doon to hire with al hire bisinesse,
Al for to make hire leve hire hevinesse.

By proces, as ye knowen everichoon,
Men may so longe graven in a stoon
Til som figure therinne emprented be.
160   So longe han they conforted hire, til she
Received hath, by hope and by resoun,
The emprenting of hire consolacioun,
Thurgh which hir grete sorwe gan aswage;
She may nat alwey duren in swich rage.

And eek Arveragus, in al this care,
Hath sent hire lettres hoom of his welfare,
And that he wol come hastily again;
Or elles hadde this sorwe hir herte slain.

Hire freendes sawe hir sorwe gan to slake,
170   And preyde hire on knees, for Goddes sake,
To come and romen hire in compaignye,
Awey to drive hire derke fantasye.
And finally she graunted that requeste,
For wel she saugh that it was for the beste.

Now stood hire castel faste by the see,
And often with hire freendes walketh shee,
Hire to disporte, upon the bank an heigh,
Where as she many a ship and barge seigh
Seillinge hir cours, where as hem liste go.
180   But thanne was that a parcel of hire wo,
For to hirself ful ofte, 'Allas!' seith she,

'Is ther no ship, of so manye as I se,
Wol bringen hom my lord? Thanne were myn herte
Al warisshed of his bittre peynes smerte.'
  Another time ther wolde she sitte and thinke,
And caste hir eyen dounward fro the brinke.
But whan she saugh the grisly rokkes blake,
For verray feere so wolde hir herte quake
That on hire feet she mighte hire noght sustene.
Thanne wolde she sitte adoun upon the grene,   190
And pitously into the see biholde,
And seyn right thus, with sorweful sikes colde:
  'Eterne God, that thurgh thy purveiaunce
Ledest the world by certein governaunce,
In idel, as men seyn, ye no thing make.
But, Lord, thise grisly feendly rokkes blake,
That semen rather a foul confusion
Of werk than any fair creacion
Of swich a parfit wys God and a stable,
Why han ye wroght this werk unresonable?   200
For by this werk, south, north, ne west, ne eest,
Ther nis yfostred man, ne brid, ne beest;
It dooth no good, to my wit, but anoyeth.
Se ye nat, Lord, how mankinde it destroyeth?
An hundred thousand bodies of mankinde
Han rokkes slain, al be they nat in minde,
Which mankinde is so fair part of thy werk
That thou it madest lyk to thyn owene merk.
Thanne semed it ye hadde a greet chiertee
Toward mankinde; but how thanne may it bee   210
That ye swiche meenes make it to destroyen,
Whiche meenes do no good, but evere anoyen?
I woot wel clerkes wol seyn as hem leste,

By argumentz, that al is for the beste,
Though I ne kan the causes nat yknowe.
But thilke God that made wind to blowe
As kepe my lord! this my conclusion.
To clerkes lete I al disputison.
But wolde God that alle thise rokkes blake
220   Were sonken into helle for his sake!
Thise rokkes sleen myn herte for the feere.'
Thus wolde she seyn, with many a pitous teere.

   Hire freendes sawe that it was no disport
To romen by the see, but disconfort,
And shopen for to pleyen somwher elles.
They leden hire by riveres and by welles,
And eek in othere places delitables;
They dauncen, and they pleyen at ches and tables.

   So on a day, right in the morwe-tide,
230   Unto a gardyn that was ther biside,
In which that they hadde maad hir ordinaunce
Of vitaille and of oother purveiaunce,
They goon and pleye hem al the longe day.
And this was on the sixte morwe of May,
Which May hadde peynted with his softe shoures
This gardyn ful of leves and of floures;
And craft of mannes hand so curiously
Arrayed hadde this gardyn, trewely,
That nevere was ther gardyn of swich prys,
240   But if it were the verray paradis.
The odour of floures and the fresshe sighte
Wolde han maked any herte lighte
That evere was born, but if to greet siknesse,
Or to greet sorwe, helde it in distresse;
So ful it was of beautee with plesaunce.

At after-diner gonne they to daunce,
And singe also, save Dorigen allone,
Which made alwey hir compleint and hir moone,
For she ne saugh him on the daunce go
That was hir housbonde and hir love also.   250
But nathelees she moste a time abide,
And with good hope lete hir sorwe slide.

   Upon this daunce, amonges othere men,
Daunced a squier biforn Dorigen,
That fressher was and jolier of array,
As to my doom, than is the month of May.
He singeth, daunceth, passinge any man
That is, or was, sith that the world bigan.
Therwith he was, if men sholde him discrive,
Oon of the beste faringe man on live;   260
Yong, strong, right vertuous, and riche, and wys,
And wel biloved, and holden in greet prys.
And shortly, if the sothe I tellen shal,
Unwiting of this Dorigen at al,
This lusty squier, servant to Venus,
Which that ycleped was Aurelius,
Hadde loved hire best of any creature
Two yeer and moore, as was his aventure,
But nevere dorste he tellen hire his grevaunce.
Withouten coppe he drank al his penaunce.   270
He was despeyred; no thing dorste he seye,
Save in his songes somwhat wolde he wreye
His wo, as in a general compleyning;
He seyde he lovede, and was biloved no thing.
Of swich matere made he manye layes,
Songes, compleintes, roundels, virelayes,
How that he dorste nat his sorwe telle,

But langwissheth as a furye dooth in helle;
And die he moste, he seyde, as dide Ekko
280 For Narcisus, that dorste nat telle hir wo.
In oother manere than ye heere me seye,
Ne dorste he nat to hire his wo biwreye,
Save that, paraventure, somtime at daunces,
Ther yonge folk kepen hir observaunces,
It may wel be he looked on hir face
In swich a wise as man that asketh grace;
But nothing wiste she of his entente.

Nathelees it happed, er they thennes wente,
By cause that he was hire neighebour,
290 And was a man of worshipe and honour,
And hadde yknowen him of time yoore,
They fille in speche; and forth, moore and moore,
Unto his purpos drough Aurelius,
And whan he saugh his time, he seyde thus:

'Madame,' quod he, 'by God that this world made,
So that I wiste it mighte youre herte glade,
I wolde that day that youre Arveragus
Wente over the see, that I, Aurelius,
Hadde went ther nevere I sholde have come again.
300 For wel I woot my service is in vain;
My gerdon is but bresting of myn herte.
Madame, reweth upon my peynes smerte;
For with a word ye may me sleen or save.
Heere at youre feet God wolde that I were grave!
I ne have as now no leiser moore to seye;
Have mercy, sweete, or ye wol do me deye.'

She gan to looke upon Aurelius:
'Is this youre wil,' quod she, 'and sey ye thus?
Nevere erst,' quod she, 'ne wiste I what ye mente.

But now, Aurelie, I knowe youre entente,   310
By thilke God that yaf me soule and lyf,
Ne shal I nevere been untrewe wyf
In word ne werk, as fer as I have wit;
I wol been his to whom that I am knit.
Taak this for final answere as of me.'
But after that in pley thus seyde she:

'Aurelie,' quod she, 'by heighe God above,
Yet wolde I graunte yow to been youre love,
Sin I yow se so pitously complaine.
Looke what day that endelong Britaine   320
Ye remoeve alle the rokkes, stoon by stoon,
That they ne lette ship ne boot to goon,—
I seye, whan ye han maad the coost so clene
Of rokkes that ther nis no stoon ysene,
Thanne wol I love yow best of any man,
Have heer my trouthe, in al that evere I kan.'

'Is ther noon oother grace in yow?' quod he.

'No, by that Lord,' quod she, 'that maked me.
For wel I woot that it shal never bitide.
Lat swiche folies out of youre herte slide.   330
What deyntee sholde a man han in his lyf
For to go love another mannes wyf,
That hath hir body whan so that him liketh?'

Aurelius ful ofte soore siketh;
Wo was Aurelie whan that he this herde,
And with a sorweful herte he thus answerde:

'Madame,' quod he, 'this were an inpossible!
Thanne moot I die of sodeyn deth horrible.'
And with that word he turned him anon.
Tho coome hir othere freendes many oon,   340
And in the aleyes romeden up and doun,

And nothing wiste of this conclusioun,
But sodeynly bigonne revel newe
Til that the brighte sonne loste his hewe;
For th'orisonte hath reft the sonne his light—
This is as muche to seye as it was night.
And hoom they goon in joye and in solas,
Save oonly wrecche Aurelius, allas!
He to his hous is goon with sorweful herte.
350 He seeth he may nat fro his deeth asterte;
Him semed that he felte his herte colde.
Up to the hevene his handes he gan holde,
And on his knowes bare he sette him doun,
And in his raving seyde his orisoun.
For verray wo out of his wit he breyde.
He niste what he spak, but thus he seyde;
With pitous herte his pleynt hath he bigonne
Unto the goddes, and first unto the sonne:
     He seyde, 'Appollo, god and governour
360 Of every plaunte, herbe, tree, and flour,
That yevest, after thy declinacion,
To ech of hem his time and his seson,
As thyn herberwe chaungeth lowe or heighe,
Lord Phebus, cast thy merciable eighe
On wrecche Aurelie, which that am but lorn.
Lo, lord! my lady hath my deeth ysworn
Withoute gilt, but thy benignitee
Upon my dedly herte have som pitee.
For wel I woot, lord Phebus, if yow lest,
370 Ye may me helpen, save my lady, best.
Now voucheth sauf that I may yow devise
How that I may been holpen and in what wise.
     Youre blisful suster, Lucina the sheene,

That of the see is chief goddesse and queene
(Though Neptunus have deitee in the see,
Yet emperisse aboven him is she),
Ye knowen wel, lord, that right as hir desir
Is to be quiked and lighted of youre fir,
For which she folweth yow ful bisily,
Right so the see desireth naturelly   380
To folwen hire, as she that is goddesse
Bothe in the see and riveres moore and lesse.
Wherfore, lord Phebus, this is my requeste—
Do this miracle, or do myn herte breste—
That now next at this opposicion
Which in the signe shal be of the Leon,
As preieth hire so greet a flood to bringe
That five fadme at the leeste it overspringe
The hyeste rokke in Armorik Briteyne;
And lat this flood endure yeres tweyne.   390
Thanne certes to my lady may I seye,
"Holdeth youre heste, the rokkes been aweye."

    Lord Phebus, dooth this miracle for me.
Preye hire she go no faster cours than ye;
I seye, preyeth your suster that she go
No faster cours than ye thise yeres two.
Thanne shal she been evene atte fulle alway,
And spring flood laste bothe night and day.
And but she vouche sauf in swich manere
To graunte me my sovereyn lady deere,   400
Prey hire to sinken every rok adoun
Into hir owene dirke regioun
Under the ground, ther Pluto dwelleth inne,
Or nevere mo shal I my lady winne.
Thy temple in Delphos wol I barefoot seke.

71

Lord Phebus, se the teeris on my cheke,
And of my peyne have som compassioun.'
And with that word in swowne he fil adoun,
And longe time he lay forth in a traunce.

410   His brother, which that knew of his penaunce,
Up caughte him, and to bedde he hath him broght.
Dispeyred in this torment and this thoght
Lete I this woful creature lie;
Chese he, for me, wheither he wol live or die.

     Arveragus, with heele and greet honour,
As he that was of chivalrie the flour,
Is comen hoom, and othere worthy men.
O blisful artow now, thou Dorigen,
That hast thy lusty housbonde in thine armes,

420   The fresshe knyght, the worthy man of armes,
That loveth thee as his owene hertes lyf.
No thing list him to been imaginatif,
If any wight hadde spoke, whil he was oute,
To hire of love; he hadde of it no doute.
He noght entendeth to no swich mateere,
But daunceth, justeth, maketh hire good cheere;
And thus in joye and blisse I lete hem dwelle,
And of the sike Aurelius wol I telle.

     In langour and in torment furius

430   Two yeer and moore lay wrecche Aurelius,
Er any foot he mighte on erthe gon;
Ne confort in this time hadde he noon,
Save of his brother, which that was a clerk.
He knew of al this wo and al this werk;
For to noon oother creature, certeyn,
Of this matere he dorste no word seyn.
Under his brest he baar it moore secree

Than evere dide Pamphilus for Galathee.
His brest was hool, withoute for to sene,
But in his herte ay was the arwe kene.   440
And wel ye knowe that of a sursanure
In surgerye is perilous the cure,
But men mighte touche the arwe, or come therby.
His brother weep and wailed prively,
Til atte laste him fil in remembraunce,
That whiles he was at Orliens in Fraunce,
As yonge clerkes, that been lykerous
To reden artes that been curious,
Seken in every halke and every herne
Particuler sciences for to lerne—   450
He him remembred that, upon a day,
At Orliens in studie a book he say
Of magik natureel, which his felawe,
That was that time a bacheler of lawe,
Al were he ther to lerne another craft,
Hadde prively upon his desk ylaft;
Which book spak muchel of the operaciouns
Touchinge the eighte and twenty mansiouns
That longen to the moone, and swich folye
As in oure dayes is nat worth a flye;   460
For hooly chirches feith in oure bileve
Ne suffreth noon illusioun us to greve.
And whan this book was in his remembraunce,
Anon for joye his herte gan to daunce,
And to himself he seyde prively:
'My brother shal be warisshed hastily;
For I am siker that ther be sciences
By whiche men make diverse apparences,
Swiche as thise subtile tregetoures pleye.

73

470 For ofte at feestes have I wel herd seye
That tregetours, withinne an halle large,
Have maad come in a water and a barge,
And in the halle rowen up and doun.
Somtime hath semed come a grim leoun;
And somtime floures springe as in a mede;
Somtime a vine, and grapes white and rede;
Somtime a castel, al of lym and stoon;
And whan hem liked, voided it anon.
Thus semed it to every mannes sighte.

480   Now thanne conclude I thus, that if I mighte
At Orliens som oold felawe yfinde
That hadde thise moones mansions in minde,
Or oother magik natureel above,
He sholde wel make my brother han his love.
For with an apparence a clerk may make,
To mannes sighte, that alle the rokkes blake
Of Britaigne weren yvoided everichon,
And shippes by the brinke comen and gon,
And in swich forme enduren a wowke or two.

490 Thanne were my brother warisshed of his wo;
Thanne moste she nedes holden hire biheste,
Or elles he shal shame hire atte leeste.'

   What sholde I make a lenger tale of this?
Unto his brotheres bed he comen is,
And swich confort he yaf him for to gon
To Orliens that he up stirte anon,
And on his wey forthward thanne is he fare
In hope for to been lissed of his care.

   Whan they were come almoost to that citee,
500 But if it were a two furlong or thre,
A yong clerk rominge by himself they mette,

Which that in Latin thriftily hem grette,
And after that he seyde a wonder thing:
'I knowe,' quod he, 'the cause of youre coming.'
And er they ferther any foote wente,
He tolde hem al that was in hire entente.

   This Briton clerk him asked of felawes
The whiche that he had knowe in olde dawes,
And he answerde him that they dede were,
For which he weep ful ofte many a teere.   510

   Doun of his hors Aurelius lighte anon,
And with this magicien forth is he gon
Hoom to his hous, and maden hem wel at ese.
Hem lakked no vitaille that mighte hem plese.
So wel arrayed hous as ther was oon
Aurelius in his lyf saugh nevere noon.

   He shewed him, er he wente to sopeer,
Forestes, parkes ful of wilde deer;
Ther saugh he hertes with hir hornes hye,
The gretteste that evere were seyn with ye.   520
He saugh of hem an hondred slain with houndes,
And somme with arwes blede of bittre woundes.
He saugh, whan voided were thise wilde deer,
Thise fauconers upon a fair river,
That with hir haukes han the heron slain.

   Tho saugh he knightes justing in a plain;
And after this he dide him swich plesaunce
That he him shewed his lady on a daunce,
On which himself he daunced, as him thoughte.
And whan this maister that this magik wroughte   530
Saugh it was time, he clapte his handes two,
And farewel! al oure revel was ago.
And yet remoeved they nevere out of the hous,

Whil they saugh al this sighte merveillous,
But in his studie, ther as his bookes be,
They seten stille, and no wight but they thre.

To him this maister called his squier,
And seyde him thus: 'Is redy oure soper?
Almoost an houre it is, I undertake,
540   Sith I yow bad oure soper for to make,
Whan that thise worthy men wenten with me
Into my studie, ther as my bookes be.'

'Sire,' quod this squier, 'whan it liketh yow,
It is al redy, though ye wol right now.'
'Go we thanne soupe,' quod he, 'as for the beste.
Thise amorous folk somtime moote han hir reste.'

At after-soper fille they in tretee
What somme sholde this maistres gerdon be,
To remoeven alle the rokkes of Britaine,
550   And eek from Gerounde to the mouth of Saine.

He made it straunge, and swoor, so God him save,
Lasse than a thousand pound he wolde nat have,
Ne gladly for that somme he wolde nat goon.

Aurelius, with blisful herte anoon,
Answerde thus: 'Fy on a thousand pound!
This wide world, which that men seye is round,
I wolde it yeve, if I were lord of it.
This bargain is ful drive, for we been knit.
Ye shal be payed trewely, by my trouthe!
560   But looketh now, for no necligence or slouthe
Ye tarie us heere no lenger than to-morwe.'

'Nay,' quod this clerk, 'have heer my feith to borwe.'

To bedde is goon Aurelius whan him leste,
And wel ny al that night he hadde his reste.

What for his labour and his hope of blisse,
His woful herte of penaunce hadde a lisse.

Upon the morwe, whan that it was day,
To Britaigne tooke they the righte way,
Aurelius and this magicien biside,
And been descended ther they wolde abide.   570
And this was, as thise bookes me remembre,
The colde, frosty seson of Decembre.

Phebus wax old, and hewed lyk laton,
That in his hoote declinacion
Shoon as the burned gold with stremes brighte;
But now in Capricorn adoun he lighte,
Where as he shoon ful pale, I dar wel seyn.
The bittre frostes, with the sleet and reyn,
Destroyed hath the grene in every yerd.
Janus sit by the fyr, with double berd,   580
And drinketh of his bugle horn the wyn;
Biforn him stant brawen of the tusked swyn,
And 'Nowel' crieth every lusty man.

Aurelius, in al that evere he kan,
Dooth to this maister chiere and reverence,
And preyeth him to doon his diligence
To bringen him out of his peynes smerte,
Or with a swerd that he wolde slitte his herte.

This subtil clerk swich routhe had of this man
That night and day he spedde him that he kan   590
To waiten a time of his conclusioun;
This is to seye, to maken illusioun,
By swich an apparence or jogelrye—
I ne kan no termes of astrologye—
That she and every wight sholde wene and seye
That of Britaigne the rokkes were aweye,

Or ellis they were sonken under grounde.
So atte laste he hath his time yfounde
To maken his japes and his wrecchednesse
600 Of swich a supersticious cursednesse.
His tables Tolletanes forth he brought,
Ful wel corrected, ne ther lakked nought,
Neither his collect ne his expans yeeris,
Ne his rootes, ne his othere geeris,
As been his centris and his argumentz
And his proporcioneles convenientz
For his equacions in every thing.
And by his eighte speere in his wirking
He knew ful wel how fer Alnath was shove
610 Fro the heed of thilke fixe Aries above,
That in the ninthe speere considered is;
Ful subtilly he kalkuled al this.

Whan he hadde founde his firste mansioun,
He knew the remenaunt by proporcioun,
And knew the arising of his moone weel,
And in whos face, and terme, and everydeel;
And knew ful weel the moones mansioun
Acordaunt to his operacioun,
And knew also his othere observaunces
620 For swiche illusiouns and swiche meschaunces
As hethen folk useden in thilke dayes.
For which no lenger maked he delayes,
But thurgh his magik, for a wyke or tweye,
It semed that alle the rokkes were aweye.

Aurelius, which that yet despeired is
Wher he shal han his love or fare amis,
Awaiteth night and day on this miracle;
And whan he knew that ther was noon obstacle,

That voided were thise rokkes everichon,
Doun to his maistres feet he fil anon,   630
And seyde, 'I woful wrecche, Aurelius,
Thanke yow, lord, and lady myn Venus,
That me han holpen fro my cares colde.'
And to the temple his wey forth hath he holde,
Where as he knew he sholde his lady see.
And whan he saugh his time, anon-right hee,
With dredful herte and with ful humble cheere,
Salewed hath his soverein lady deere:
  'My righte lady,' quod this woful man,
'Whom I moost drede and love as I best kan,   640
And lothest were of al this world displese,
Nere it that I for yow have swich disese
That I moste dien heere at youre foot anon,
Noght wolde I telle how me is wo bigon.
But certes outher moste I die or pleyne;
Ye sle me giltelees for verray peyne.
But of my deeth thogh that ye have no routhe,
Aviseth yow er that ye breke youre trouthe.
Repenteth yow, for thilke God above,
Er ye me sleen by cause that I yow love.   650
For, madame, wel ye woot what ye han hight—
Nat that I chalange any thing of right
Of yow, my soverein lady, but youre grace—
But in a gardyn yond, at swich a place,
Ye woot right wel what ye bihighten me;
And in myn hand youre trouthe plighten ye
To love me best—God woot, ye seyde so,
Al be that I unworthy am therto.
Madame, I speke it for the honour of yow
Moore than to save myn hertes lyf right now,—   660

I have do so as ye comanded me;
And if ye vouche sauf, ye may go see.
Dooth as yow list; have youre biheste in minde,
For, quik or deed, right there ye shal me finde.
In yow lith al to do me live or deye,—
But wel I woot the rokkes been aweye.'

He taketh his leve, and she astoned stood;
In al hir face nas a drope of blood.
She wende nevere han come in swich a trappe.
670   'Allas,' quod she, 'that evere this sholde happe!
For wende I nevere by possibilitee
That swich a monstre or merveille mighte be!
It is agains the proces of nature.'
And hoom she goth a sorweful creature;
For verray feere unnethe may she go.
She wepeth, wailleth, al a day or two,
And swowneth, that it routhe was to see.
But why it was to no wight tolde shee,
For out of towne was goon Arveragus.
680   But to hirself she spak, and seyde thus,
With face pale and with ful sorweful cheere,
In hire compleynt, as ye shal after heere:

'Allas,' quod she, 'on thee, Fortune, I pleyne,
That unwar wrapped hast me in thy cheyne,
Fro which t'escape woot I no socour,
Save oonly deeth or elles dishonour;
Oon of thise two bihoveth me to chese.
But nathelees, yet have I levere to lese
My lyf than of my body to have a shame,
690   Or knowe myselven fals, or lese my name;
And with my deth I may be quit, ywis.
Hath ther nat many a noble wyf er this,

And many a maide, yslain hirself, allas!
Rather than with hir body doon trespas?
    Yis, certes, lo, thise stories beren witnesse:
Whan thritty tirauntz, ful of cursednesse,
Hadde slain Phidon in Atthenes atte feste,
They comanded his doghtres for t'areste,
And bringen hem biforn hem in despit,
Al naked, to fulfille hir foul delit,   700
And in hir fadres blood they made hem daunce
Upon the pavement, God yeve hem meschaunce!
For which thise woful maidens, ful of drede,
Rather than they wolde lese hir maidenhede,
They prively been stirt into a welle,
And dreynte hemselven, as the bookes telle.
    They of Mecene leete enquere and seke
Of Lacedomye fifty maidens eke,
On whiche they wolden doon hir lecherye.
But was ther noon of al that compaignye   710
That she nas slain, and with a good entente
Chees rather for to die than assente
To been oppressed of hir maidenhede.
Why sholde I thanne to die been in drede?
Lo, eek, the tiraunt Aristoclides,
That loved a maiden, heet Stymphalides,
Whan that hir fader slain was on a night,
Unto Dianes temple goth she right,
And hente the image in hir handes two,
Fro which image wolde she nevere go.   720
No wight ne mighte hir handes of it arace
Til she was slain, right in the selve place.
    Now sith that maidens hadden swich despit
To been defouled with mannes foul delit,

Wel oghte a wyf rather hirselven slee
Than be defouled, as it thinketh me.
What shal I seyn of Hasdrubales wyf,
That at Cartage birafte hirself hir lyf?
For whan she saugh that Romayns wan the toun,
730   She took hir children alle, and skipte adoun
Into the fyr, and chees rather to die
Than any Romayn dide hire vileynye.
Hath nat Lucresse yslain hirself, allas!
At Rome, whan that she oppressed was
Of Tarquin, for hire thoughte it was a shame
To liven whan that she had lost hir name?
The sevene maidens of Milesie also
Han slain hemself, for verrey drede and wo,
Rather than folk of Gawle hem sholde oppresse.
740   Mo than a thousand stories, as I gesse,
Koude I now telle as touchinge this mateere.
Whan Habradate was slain, his wyf so deere
Hirselven slow, and leet hir blood to glide
In Habradates woundes depe and wide,
And seyde, "My body, at the leeste way,
Ther shal no wight defoulen, if I may."
    What sholde I mo ensamples heerof sayn,
Sith that so manye han hemselven slain
Wel rather than they wolde defouled be?
750   I wol conclude that it is bet for me
To sleen myself than been defouled thus.
I wol be trewe unto Arveragus,
Or rather sleen myself in som manere,
As dide Demociones doghter deere
By cause that she wolde nat defouled be.
O Cedasus, it is ful greet pitee

To reden how thy doghtren deyde, allas!
That slowe hemself for swich a manere cas.
As greet a pitee was it, or wel moore,
The Theban maiden that for Nichanore   760
Hirselven slow, right for swich manere wo.
Another Theban maiden dide right so;
For oon of Macidonye hadde hire oppressed,
She with hire deeth hir maidenhede redressed.
What shal I seye of Nicerates wyf,
That for swich cas birafte hirself hir lyf?
How trewe eek was to Alcebiades
His love, that rather for to dien chees
Than for to suffre his body unburied be.
Lo, which a wyf was Alceste,' quod she.   770
'What seith Omer of goode Penalopee?
Al Grece knoweth of hire chastitee.
Pardee, of Laodomya is writen thus,
That whan at Troie was slain Protheselaus,
Ne lenger wolde she live after his day.
The same of noble Porcia telle I may;
Withoute Brutus koude she nat live,
To whom she hadde al hool hir herte yive.
The parfit wyfhod of Arthemesie
Honured is thurgh al the Barbarie.   780
O Teuta, queene! thy wyfly chastitee
To alle wives may a mirour bee.
The same thing I seye of Bilyea,
Of Rodogone, and eek Valeria.'

    Thus pleyned Dorigen a day or tweye,
Purposinge evere that she wolde deye.
But nathelees, upon the thridde night,
Hoom cam Arveragus, this worthy knight,

And asked hire why that she weep so soore;
790   And she gan wepen ever lenger the moore.
'Allas,' quod she, 'that evere was I born!
Thus have I seyd,' quod she, 'thus have I sworn'—
And toold him al as ye han herd bifore;
It nedeth nat reherce it yow namoore.
This housbonde, with glad chiere, in freendly wise
Answerde and seyde as I shal yow devise:
'Is ther oght elles, Dorigen, but this?'
  'Nay, nay,' quod she, 'God helpe me so as wys!
This is to muche, and it were Goddes wille.'
800   'Ye, wyf,' quod he, 'lat slepen that is stille.
It may be wel, paraventure, yet to day.
Ye shul youre trouthe holden, by my fay!
For God so wisly have mercy upon me,
I hadde wel levere ystiked for to be
For verray love which that I to yow have,
But if ye sholde youre trouthe kepe and save.
Trouthe is the hyeste thing that man may kepe'—
But with that word he brast anon to wepe,
And seyde, 'I yow forbede, up peyne of deeth,
810   That nevere, whil thee lasteth lyf ne breeth,
To no wight telle thou of this aventure—
As I may best, I wol my wo endure—
Ne make no contenance of hevinesse,
That folk of yow may demen harm or gesse.'
  And forth he cleped a squier and a maide:
'Gooth forth anon with Dorigen,' he saide,
'And bringeth hire to swich a place anon.'
They take hir leve, and on hir wey they gon,
But they ne wiste why she thider wente.
820   He nolde no wight tellen his entente.

Paraventure an heep of yow, ywis,
Wol holden him a lewed man in this
That he wol putte his wyf in jupartie.
Herkneth the tale er ye upon hire crie.
She may have bettre fortune than yow semeth;
And whan that ye han herd the tale, demeth.

This squier, which that highte Aurelius,
On Dorigen that was so amorus,
Of aventure happed hire to meete
Amidde the toun, right in the quikkest strete,   830
As she was bown to goon the wey forth right
Toward the gardyn ther as she had hight.
And he was to the gardyn-ward also;
For wel he spied whan she wolde go
Out of hir hous to any maner place.
But thus they mette, of aventure or grace,
And he saleweth hire with glad entente,
And asked of hire whiderward she wente;
And she answerde, half as she were mad,
'Unto the gardyn, as myn housbonde bad,   840
My trouthe for to holde, allas! allas!'

Aurelius gan wondren on this cas,
And in his herte hadde greet compassioun
Of hire and of hire lamentacioun,
And of Arveragus, the worthy knight,
That bad hire holden al that she had hight,
So looth him was his wyf sholde breke hir trouthe;
And in his herte he caughte of this greet routhe,
Consideringe the beste on every side,
That fro his lust yet were him levere abide   850
Than doon so heigh a cherlissh wrecchednesse
Agains franchise and alle gentillesse;

For which in fewe wordes seyde he thus:
  'Madame, seyth to youre lord Arveragus
That sith I se his grete gentillesse
To yow, and eek I se wel youre distresse,
That him were levere han shame (and that were
    routhe)
Than ye to me sholde breke thus youre trouthe,
I have wel levere evere to suffre wo
Than I departe the love bitwix yow two.
I yow relesse, madame, into youre hond
Quit every serement and every bond
That ye han maad to me as heerbiforn,
Sith thilke time which that ye were born.
My trouthe I plighte, I shal yow never repreve
Of no biheste, and heere I take my leve,
As of the treweste and the beste wyf
That evere yet I knew in al my lyf.
But every wyf be war of hire biheeste!
On Dorigen remembreth, atte leeste.
Thus kan a squier doon a gentil dede
As wel as kan a knight, withouten drede.'

  She thonketh him upon hir knees al bare,
And hoom unto hir housbonde is she fare,
And tolde him al, as ye han herd me said;
And be ye siker, he was so weel apayd
That it were inpossible me to write.
What sholde I lenger of this cas endite?
  Arveragus and Dorigen his wyf
In soverein blisse leden forth hir lyf.
Nevere eft ne was ther angre hem bitwene.
He cherisseth hire as though she were a queene,
And she was to him trewe for everemoore.

Of thise two folk ye gete of me namoore.

   Aurelius, that his cost hath al forlorn,
Curseth the time that evere he was born:
'Allas,' quod he, 'allas, that I bihighte
Of pured gold a thousand pound of wighte
Unto this philosophre! How shal I do?
I se namoore but that I am fordo.   890
Myn heritage moot I nedes selle,
And been a beggere; heere may I nat dwelle,
And shamen al my kinrede in this place,
But I of him may gete bettre grace.
But nathelees, I wole of him assaye,
At certeyn dayes, yeer by yeer, to paye,
And thanke him of his grete curteisye.
My trouthe wol I kepe, I wol nat lie.'

   With herte soor he gooth unto his cofre,
And broghte gold unto this philosophre,   900
The value of five hundred pound, I gesse,
And him bisecheth, of his gentillesse,
To graunte him dayes of the remenaunt;
And seyde, 'Maister, I dar wel make avaunt,
I failled nevere of my trouthe as yit.
For sikerly my dette shal be quit
Towardes yow, howevere that I fare,
To goon a-begged in my kirtle bare.
But wolde ye vouche sauf, upon seuretee,
Two yeer or thre for to respiten me,   910
Thanne were I wel; for elles moot I selle
Myn heritage; ther is namoore to telle.'

   This philosophre sobrely answerde,
And seyde thus, whan he thise wordes herde:
'Have I nat holden covenant unto thee?'

'Yes, certes, wel and trewely,' quod he.
'Hastow nat had thy lady as thee liketh?'
'No, no,' quod he, and sorwefully he siketh.
'What was the cause? tel me if thou kan.'
920   Aurelius his tale anon bigan,
And tolde him al, as ye han herd bifoore;
It nedeth nat to yow reherce it moore.

He seide, 'Arveragus, of gentillesse,
Hadde levere die in sorwe and in distresse
Than that his wyf were of hir trouthe fals.'
The sorwe of Dorigen he tolde him als;
How looth hire was to been a wikked wyf,
And that she levere had lost that day hir lyf,
And that hir trouthe she swoor thurgh innocence,—
930   She nevere erst hadde herd speke of apparence.
'That made me han of hire so greet pitee;
And right as frely as he sente hire me,
As frely sente I hire to him ageyn.
This al and som; ther is namoore to seyn.'

This philosophre answerde, 'Leeve brother,
Everich of yow dide gentilly til oother.
Thou art a squier and he is a knight;
But God forbede, for his blisful might,
But if a clerk koude doon a gentil dede
940   As wel as any of yow, it is no drede!
Sire, I releesse thee thy thousand pound,
As thou right now were cropen out of the ground,
Ne nevere er now ne haddest knowen me.
For, sire, I wol nat taken a peny of thee
For al my craft, ne noght for my travaille.
Thou hast ypayed wel for my vitaille.
It is ynogh, and farewel, have good day!'

And took his hors, and forth he goth his way.
Lordinges, this question, thanne, wol I aske now,
Which was the mooste fre, as thinketh yow?   950
Now telleth me, er that ye ferther wende.
I kan namoore; my tale is at an ende.

NOTES

1–2. The Squire, the son of the Knight, has been telling a long and excessively complicated story belonging to the genre of chivalric romance. The Franklin interrupts him in mid-senter.ce just as he has summarized the further complications still to come, but he does so with the greatest possible politeness. For more detailed comment, see Introduction, pp. 5–8.

2. *gentilly* From the very beginning, the Franklin introduces, as part of his compliment to the Squire, the concept of *gentillesse* which is to be a key element in his own story.

4. *allow the* 'praise thee'. Note the rhyme *yowthe . . . allow the*, which forms part of the evidence for supposing that the final *-e*, though mute in fourteenth-century speech, was pronounced at the end of a line of Chaucerian verse.

8. *vertu* Probably with a somewhat wider sense than 'virtue' today, meaning manly qualities in general, and thus recalling the etymology from Latin *virtus* (cf. *vir*, 'man').

11. *twenty pound worth lond* 'land worth twenty pounds a year in rent'.

12. 'Though it had come into my possession at this very moment.'

16. *yet shal* 'shall continue to do so'.

23. This forthright manner of talking is characteristic of Harry Bailly, the host of the Tabard Inn, who had been appointed master of ceremonies for the journey by the other pilgrims. The Franklin has already used *gentil*, *gentilly*, and *gentillesse* once each, not to mention *vertu* (twice) and *vertuous*, and the Host fears that he may be embarking on a moral disquisition rather than a story.

24–6. The original proposal, made by the Host and agreed to by the other pilgrims, was that each of them should tell two tales on the way to Canterbury and two on the way back. If this had been carried out, it would have resulted in an enormous collection of some 120 stories. The vagueness here about the number of tales to be told by each pilgrim may be a sign that, as he proceeded with the work, Chaucer was coming to feel that the original scheme was impossible.

46. *have me excused of* 'allow me to be excused for'.

47. *rethorik* Rhetoric was the art of eloquence, and played an important part in medieval education. See Introduction, pp. 17–18.

49–54. For comment and explanation, see Introduction, pp. 18–19.

57. *Armorik* Armorica, a learned name for Brittany. This line helps to set the tale in the pagan past: it 'is' (i.e. now) called Brittany.

61. *were* Subjunctive, because the outcome was uncertain.

62. *oon the faireste under sonne* An emphatic form of the superlative: 'one who was the most beautiful on earth' not 'one of the most beautiful on earth'.

63. 'And, moreover, descended from such an aristocratic family.'

64. *wel* This adds emphasis to *unnethes*, 'hardly', but cannot be translated in modern English.

68. 'Took such pity on his suffering.'

71. The line may be intended to have a sardonic ring, reflecting on the extreme theories, of male dominance and female dominance respectively, of the Clerk and the Wife of Bath.

72. 'And so as to lead their lives in greater happiness.'

73. *as a knight* 'by his knighthood'.

75. *maistrie* was a word much used by the Wife of Bath to describe the relationship between husband and wife, as was *soverainetee* (line 79 below).

78. See Introduction, pp. 29–30.

80. 'Out of regard for his rank.' Presumably the *degree* concerned is that of husband, though conceivably it might be that of knight, by which he has just sworn. The Franklin is extremely conscious of social position (as in his emphasis on the lady's high rank).

83–5. 'You propose to allow me to rule so freely, may God never permit that there should be either hostility or quarrelling between the two of us through any fault of mine.'

87. *trouthe* The first mention of a concept that is to be very important in *The Franklin's Tale*.

89–114. A digression, in which the Franklin offers his own views on the way in which marriage may best be arranged so as to allow for inevitable human frailties. Digression is encouraged by the medieval *artes poeticae* as a means of amplifying a given story, and many of the *Canterbury Tales* include such digressions shortly after the narrative itself has begun. Their purpose is to lay explicit stress on themes which will emerge as the meaning of the story.

90. *freendes* 'lovers'.

93–4. The sudden change from abstractions such as *maistrye* to this vividly realized personification is startlingly effective. The god of love—Cupid, the son of Venus—was usually represented as winged. In the Middle Ages he is usually shown in literature as himself exercising *maistrye* over lovers.

96. *of kinde* 'by nature'.

99. *looke who* 'whoever'.

100. 'In a position of complete superiority.' The paradox is sharp: perhaps too sharp, for it does not get rid of *maistrye* but suggests a different way of achieving it.

102–3. 'For, as the scholars say, it overcomes in matters where severity would never be successful.' There is no need to identify *thise clerkes*, for it is common in medieval literature to attribute such general statements about human life (*sententiae*) to the learned. Statements making this particular point are common from the Bible onwards.

104. 'One can't scold or complain for every little word.'

105. *so moot I goon* 'I assure you'—a common and almost meaningless asseveration, literally 'As I hope to live'.

108. *that he ne dooth* 'who does not do'.

109. *constellacioun* The position of the planets in relation to each other, which was believed to influence human life. Translate 'planetary influence'.

110. *complexioun* The balance of the four humours in a person's body, which were believed to govern the health and disposition.

113–14. 'Anyone who is capable of self-control will restrain himself according to the occasion.'

115. Here the Franklin returns to his story, though he still has more discursive matter about marriage to offer before the actual narrative can continue.

120–6. The paradoxical nature of their marriage is further asserted. According to *fine amour* (which was theoretically supposed to exist only outside marriage) the woman had absolute dominion; according to marriage, as conceived in the Middle Ages, the man had absolute dominion. In this marriage, the two relationships are combined.

123. *lordshipe above* 'supreme dominion'.

126. 'With which the law of love is in agreement.'

131–4. These lines, both verbally and in their interrogative form, echo a passage in *The Merchant's Tale*. (See Introduction, p. 29.)

135. The second *of* is redundant.

136. *Kayrrud* This seems to be a phonetic spelling of a genuine fourteenth-century place-name, which has now become 'Kerru'. There is more than one Kerru in Brittany, but none in the exact region where the Tale is set.

    Arveragus A Celtic name, given in a Latinized form.

138. In the Middle Ages Brittany was often called Little Britain, as opposed to Great Britain. Britain is an archaic and scholarly name for England, as Armorica for Brittany.

140. The Franklin is here repeating a chivalric theme from *The Squire's Tale*, where a female falcon tells of how she was courted by a male and accepted his advances, and how he then said he must leave her to pursue honour. In medieval chivalric romances it is generally agreed that a knight must not linger at home, even though married, but must go off in search of martial adventure.

141. *the book seith thus* There is no reason to suppose that the Franklin, or Chaucer, is really referring to a particular book. Medieval poets usually pretended to be following some authoritative source, even when they were not.

143. *Dorigen* Another Celtic name, probably pronounced with a hard *g*.

146. The tone of this line is highly dubious: is the Franklin showing a naïf admiration for the capacity of the aristocracy to express intense emotions, or is he sardonically suggesting that noble wives have their sighing and weeping thoroughly under control?

147. Intense emotions, and especially intense grief, tend to be expressed in medieval poetry in a formalized, non-realistic way, and this line sums up the usual external symptoms of misery: yearning, wailing, lamenting, and an inability to sleep or eat.

151. *in al that ever they may* 'in every way they possibly can'.

157–9. These lines form a *sententia* which is also a miniature digression, whose connexion with the main line of the narrative does not become apparent until the transition in line

160. The saying that 'long dripping wears away the hardest stone' is a common one, and occurs in Boccaccio's *Filocolo*, a probable source for *The Franklin's Tale*. But this is not exactly what the Franklin says, and it has been pointed out (by M. J. Donovan, *Journal of English and Germanic Philology*, LVI [1957]) that a closer parallel is found in the *Anticlaudianus* of Alain de Lille, a medieval Latin poem which was known to Chaucer.

172. *derke fantasye* Fantasye is also treated as dangerous in *The Merchant's Tale*: there lustful imaginings are concerned, here melancholic imaginings.

182. *of so manye as I se* 'among all those I see'.

184. 'Completely cured of the pain of its bitter sorrow.'

206. *al be they nat in minde* 'although they are forgotten'.

208. *lyk to thyn owene merk* 'in thine own image'—repeating the language of Gen. i. 27, where the Latin *imago* is used. This is one of the basic texts for medieval Christian thought about the nature of man.

217. *as kepe* 'may (God) preserve'. The *as* is a normal means of expressing a wish or hope in Middle English.

   this my conclusion 'this is *my* conclusion'. Dorigen is parodying the technical philosophical language which she attributes to *clerkes*.

222. This line has the explicitness that belongs to a poetry intended for reading aloud to a listening audience. In such poetry, the author, to make sure that the listeners (who will not possess a written text of the work) will be able to follow it, will need first to say what he is going to do (as in line 192) and then to say when he has done it.

227. *delitables* The adjective is derived from French, and it is under French influence that it agrees in number with the noun.

228. *tables* 'backgammon'—a game of chance played with dice.

229. Here begins a separate scene in the poem, in striking contrast to the previous one. For the terrifying rocky landscape of the coast is substituted the paradisal landscape of an enclosed garden. For comment, see Introduction, pp. 41–2.

234. May is the season in which the symbolic garden of love is usually described (as it is in the *Roman de la Rose*, for example), but it is not known what special significance, if any, the date of the sixth may have had for Chaucer.

235. 'And May with its gentle showers had painted.' The metaphor of painting is common in medieval descriptions of spring.

237. *craft of mannes hand* 'human skill'—nature and art combine to make the garden seductively beautiful.

246. Dinner in the Middle Ages would have been at midday or earlier.

260. The construction here is a confusion of that found in line 62 with the more familiar 'one of the handsomest men'.

261. *vertuous* See note on line 8.

265. *lusty* Contrary to what the context may suggest, this does not mean 'lustful' or even 'virile' but simply 'pleasant'.

    servant to Venus Venus is the goddess of love. Love relationships are commonly seen in the Middle Ages in feudal terms, so that the lover becomes the 'servant' of Venus or Cupid, or of his lady. It is precisely this feudalization from which the Franklin seems to be trying to escape in his description of the relationship between Dorigen and Arveragus.

266. *Aurelius* A Roman name, which was used in Roman Britain.

269–80. Unaccepted love is normally described in medieval courtly literature as a state of intense anguish or *penaunce*. It is literally a disease, which if uncured may lead to madness and death. The symptoms are further described below, in lines 429–43.

270. *withouten coppe* A cryptic phrase, whose meaning has not been definitely ascertained. Perhaps the most likely is that suggested by Professor Hodgson in her edition of *The Franklin's Tale*: 'without measure, i.e. not in measured doses, but from the fountain head'.

271. *despeyred* 'in despair'. The word has theological overtones, despair of God's grace being the ultimate sin, which makes salvation impossible. *Fine amour* is often developed into a pseudo-theology, secular love being seen as a parallel to or parody of divine love. Grace is what the lover hopes to gain from his lady (compare line 286).

273. *general compleyning* 'lament in general terms'.

275. *matere* A little more specific in meaning than the modern 'matter'; it is the regular word for the subject-matter of literature as opposed to its form.

    layes 'songs'—a more general sense than in 'Breton Lays', which are narrative poems.

276. The *compleint* or lament was a common medieval literary genre. Chaucer, in his capacity as court poet, wrote a number of *compleintes*. *Roundels* and *virelayes* are both short poems whose form is based on round dances, the verses being sung by an individual and followed by refrains sung by the whole company. Their fixed form and repeated rhymes gave scope for the virtuosity that was expected of a courtier.

278. The three Furies in classical mythology were spirits which tormented the souls there, but Chaucer seems to have thought of them as suffering pain themselves.

279–80. Echo was a nymph who fell in love with the handsome youth Narcissus, and, when he did not return her love, wasted away until she became only a repeating voice. The story is told by Ovid in the *Metamorphoses*. The Franklin (or Chaucer over the Franklin's shoulder) may have chosen this particular comparison as a sign of the effeminacy to which Aurelius is reduced by love.

284. Customary social events such as the ceremonies of May day or Christmas, or even as here dances, are often referred to as *observaunces*.

291. *hadde* 'she had'.

295. The oath reminds us of Dorigen's anguish about the rationale of the divine creation, and prepares us for the reintroduction of the rocks.

300. *service* 'devotion'—compare note on *servant to Venus* in line 265.

305. *as* Redundant (as frequently in Middle English).

316–26. Here Dorigen makes her fatal mistake, in a way that is all the more humanly convincing because it is unintentional and yet reveals her deepest feelings. She has too much feminine soft-heartedness to be able to hurt Aurelius (who, after all, has just declared that he loves her) by an unqualified refusal, and so she reverts from being an outraged wife to playing the part of the courtly mistress that her marriage has left open to her. Her device for evading a direct refusal will work only on condition that the task really is impossible. If it were to be performed, the very event that would open the way for her husband's safe return would also give her lover the right to possess her. And what would happen then?

320. *looke what day* 'whatever day'.

328–33. Here Dorigen reverts to the role of faithful wife, and

in lines 331–3 she specifically repudiates the courtly convention, by which love could only occur outside marriage.

337–9. There is perhaps an intentional note of melodrama in
Aurelius's words and action, though, as has been mentioned,
love was thought of as a disease that really could lead to death.
However, there is no question of *sodeyn* (immediate) death,
however *horrible*, for we later learn that Aurelius languishes
in misery for over two years.

340. Again a skilful change of scene, with the sudden appearance
of her friends, gaily ignorant of the drama that has just
occurred and of Aurelius's misery.

344–6. For comment on these lines, see Introduction, p. 21.

348. Another sudden shift to a scene of contrasting emotion.

351. *colde* Verb, not adjective.

359–407. The setting of the tale is pagan, and so Aurelius prays
not to the Christian God, but to the sun-god of classical
paganism, Apollo. But the mythological detail of this speech
is not merely antiquarianism on Chaucer's part, for the
classical gods had become attached to particular 'planets'
(including the sun and moon), and in the Christian Middle
Ages they retained a genuine power through the belief in
astrology. For more detailed comment on this, see *An Introduction to Chaucer*, ch. 6, and *The Knight's Tale*, ed. Spearing,
pp. 54–65. In this speech there is some genuine science mixed
in with the pseudo-science of astrology, for of course the
movements of the sea are influenced by the moon.

An invocation similar to this occurs in the *Teseida* of Boccaccio, but Chaucer may also have been influenced by the
passage of Boethius used in Dorigen's earlier invocation of
God. This passage (Book I, metrum 5) is concerned with the
regularity of times and seasons: it addresses God as *governour*
(cf. line 359), speaks of *seedes*, *leeves*, and *cornes* (cf. line 360),
and begins with a reference to the moon and *hir brother*
(cf. line 373) the sun.

For further comment on this speech, see Introduction,
p. 40.

364. *Phebus* Phoebus is a name applied to Apollo in his role
as sun-god.

365. *which that am but lorn* 'who am utterly lost'.

367. *withoute gilt* 'without any fault of mine'. *but* 'unless'
(followed by a verb in the subjunctive, *have* not *hath*).

benignitee Apollo, according to medieval astrology, was the most favourable of the planet-gods in influence, and was therefore sometimes called *Fortuna major*.

373. *Lucina* One of the names of the threefold goddess Diana. She is Diana, the goddess of hunting and chastity on earth, Luna, the moon, in heaven, and Proserpina in the underworld. As Lucina she is the goddess prayed to for help by women in childbirth. For further information, see *The Knight's Tale*, ed. Spearing, lines 1193–228 (the description of the temple of Diana). It has been suggested that Aurelius has to adopt the roundabout approach of asking Apollo to ask his sister to make the sea rise because he knew that, as Diana, she was the goddess of chastity, and would have been unlikely to perform a miracle to enable him to seduce another man's wife.

375–6. Neptune was the god of the sea itself, but the sea's movements were controlled by the influence of the moon.

377–8. The moon shines with light reflected from the sun. This scientific fact was known in the Middle Ages, but it is interesting to see here how it is humanized, and made a matter not simply of neutral reflexion but of desire and the kindling of fire.

379. This presumably refers to the fact that night continually succeeds day, and so the moon the sun.

385–6. *The Leon* is Leo, the lion, one of the twelve 'houses' of the zodiac, the belt across the sky within which the sun and the other planets move in their courses. The sun is especially associated with the house of Leo, and is at its most powerful when within it. In May, when Aurelius makes his prayer, the sun is in another house, Taurus, the bull, and he will have to wait three months for the sun to be in Leo. At that time the moon will be 'in opposition' to the sun (that is, they will be 180 degrees apart at full moon), and this is one of the arrangements which causes the tides to be highest, because the sun influences them as well as the moon.

387. *as* See note on line 217.

393. What has been requested so far is in the course of nature, but what Aurelius goes on to ask for is indeed a miracle, for it involves making the moon move at the same apparent rate as the sun for two years (i.e. revolving round the earth once a year instead of once a month), so as to keep the same

exceptional spring tide in being. His science appears to be mistaken, however, for this miracle would not produce the effect he desires.

399. *but she vouche sauf* 'if she will not consent'.

401–3. This will be within her powers as Proserpina or Hecate, goddess of the underworld, which is ruled over by the god Pluto.

405. *Delphos* A confusion of Delos, where Apollo was born, and Delphi, where his chief oracle was. Aurelius, in medieval fashion, is vowing a barefoot 'pilgrimage' to this shrine if his prayer is answered.

413. *lete I...lie* 'I leave...lying'.

414. 'So far as I am concerned, he can make up his own mind whether he is going to live or die.'

438. *Pamphilus* and *Galathee* (Galatea) are characters in a medieval Latin poetic dialogue, *Pamphilus de Amore*.

439–43. The metaphor of love as a wound received in the breast (or heart) from an arrow is common in medieval courtly poetry. It is found in the influential *Roman de la Rose*, and also in the opening lines of *Pamphilus de Amore*. It is often treated literally, so that, as here, the means of curing the wound can be discussed in technical medical terms. Thus the *sursanure*, or wound healed over on the surface, becomes an image for the passion of love kept secret.

445–56. The Franklin is trying to convey too much information in a single sentence, and changes grammatical construction (drawing breath, as it were) halfway through.

446. *Orliens in Fraunce* Brittany was a duchy separate from France in Chaucer's time, but Bretons used regularly to go and study at the University of Orleans.

448. 'To study esoteric sciences.' At universities today, students are still spoken of as 'reading' particular subjects, not 'studying' them. This is the first suggestion of magic in the poem.

451. *Remembred* is here used as a reflexive verb; compare modern French *il se souvint*.

452. *at Orliens in studie* 'while he was studying at Orleans'.

453. *magik natureel* There was a clear distinction in the Middle Ages between 'natural magic' and necromancy or 'black magic'. Natural magic was a science which brought power through a special knowledge of natural phenomena (such as,

in this case, planetary influences), while necromancy made use of evil spirits, and was universally condemned.

454. *bacheler of lawe* An advanced student who has not yet taken his master's degree. Orleans was famous for the study of law in the Middle Ages, but it was also known as a centre of astrology.

457–9. The twenty-eight *mansiouns* of the moon are the positions in which it appears on each of the twenty-eight days of the lunar month. In each position it had a different kind of influence, and so a knowledge of these positions was of great value for someone who wished to predict or change the future.

459–62. Another withdrawal from involvement in the tale: we are reminded that we are Christians, while the tale belongs to the errors of a pagan past. If we think of this remark as being the Franklin's, it sounds perhaps somewhat anxious—he is concerned to assert his own respectable orthodoxy. If we think of it as Chaucer's, it takes on a more quizzical air, a little sceptical that *hooly chirches feith* is so all-powerful. The Wife of Bath at the beginning of her tale makes some similar remarks about how the *grete charitee and prayeres* of the friars have abolished fairies, and these too must be understood ironically.

461. 'For the faith of Holy Church in our creed.'

470–9. Conjuring tricks of this kind were used as entertainments at feasts in Chaucer's time.

470–1. *for ofte...that tregetours* 'for I have certainly heard it said that often at feasts conjurers'.

479. This line emphasizes the element of seeming in magic; the changes caused by magicians only appear to be so.

481. *oold felawe* 'former companion (of mine)'.

485–6. Further emphasis on the illusory nature of magic.

493. Such indications that the writer intends to be brief are very common in Chaucer and other medieval poets. The *artes poeticae* sometimes divide the possible purposes of poetry into two, to amplify the given material and to abbreviate it, and the poets tend to be very conscious which of the two they are doing. The following sentence is indeed extraordinarily concise; in line 494 he is still approaching his brother's bed with his new idea, and in line 498 the two of them are already on the way to Orleans to carry it out.

Notes

500. 'No more than some two or three furlongs away.' A furlong is one-eighth of a mile.

507–8. The brother is hoping to carry out his original plan (lines 480–1) of making contact with some former friend of his who knows about natural magic.

513. *maden hem* 'they made themselves'.

515–16. 'Never in his life had Aurelius seen a house so well arranged as that one was.'

517–29. For comment, see Introduction, pp. 52–3.

529. *as him thoughte* 'as it seemed to him'. Again the emphasis on the illusory nature of magic, now at a crucial point, when Aurelius seems to be achieving what he most desires.

535. *ther as his bookes be* This clause, as its recurrence in line 542 indicates, is little more than the kind of time- and space-filler that belongs to the diffuse style of a poem intended for oral delivery. But, though a formula, it has a certain significance here, for it is presumably his books that have enabled him to create the illusions.

545. *as for the beste* 'as the best thing to do'. Another space-filler.

546. *thise amorous folk* 'people in love'.

550. The Gironde and the Seine are rivers almost equally far from Penmarc'h on opposite sides.

551. *so God him save* 'as he hoped to be saved'—a common oath.

556. It was regularly taught in the Middle Ages that the earth was round, not flat.

562. *have heer my feith to borwe* 'take my promise as a pledge'. They make their agreement with legal formality.

571. *thise bookes* See note on line 141.

573–83. These lines, deriving from a literary and rhetorical tradition, form an extremely elaborate periphrasis for the statement that it was in December. But they are also related to a visual tradition. They form a literary equivalent for the illuminations in medieval Calendars and Books of Hours (the best known example today being probably *Les Très Riches Heures du Duc de Berry*), in which the upper part of the picture will show the astronomical situation for a month (lines 573–7), while the lower part will contain a typical scene from life in the same month (lines 578–83). Janus is the god of the turn of the year, and he is sometimes shown in illustrations of January (the month called after him) but sometimes also in those of December. The feasting scene is shown in illustrations of several winter months, but is particularly appropriate to the Christmas feast, which in medieval times lasted from 25 December to 6 January. Thus the rhetorical significance of this passage is clear, and so is its imaginative vitality: it stands out from its surroundings as brilliantly coloured and full of vigorous life. What is not clear is its function at this point in the poem. It seems possible to see it as representing a promise that the forces of evil or illusion will not win: even in the *colde, frosty seson of Decembre,* so ominously chosen for the experiment, a vigorous and familiarly English life survives. But equally Janus *with double berd* is a fundamentally ambiguous figure, looking both back and forward, hinting perhaps at both good and evil.

573–7. In summer the sun shines powerfully from a high altitude (*declinacion*) in the sky; at the winter solstice, when it is in the zodiacal house of Capricorn (compare note on lines 385–6), it is duller in colour and shines only palely.

580. *with double berd* Janus is often shown with two faces looking in opposite directions. Here these are merely alluded to in the double beard, and he becomes a hearty human figure, perhaps in the image of the Franklin himself, who was much given to good food.

581. *bugle horn* The horn of the bugle or wild ox was used as a drinking vessel.

582. A boar's head was a ceremonial dish for Christmas festivities, and is also often shown in January illuminations in medieval Calendars.

583. *Nowel* (from Latin *natalis*, 'birthday') was shouted aloud at the Christmas festivities.

588. 'Or (he said) that he would pierce his own heart with a sword.'

591. 'To be on the watch for an opportunity for his experiment.'

594. With this modest parenthesis, compare the *diminutio* in lines 44–55. As there, it is immediately followed by an ostentatious display of knowledge. Here, though, it is only the *termes* of astrology of which knowledge is shown: the Franklin can produce a great flow of its jargon, but seems to know little of its operations in detail.

600. *supersticious* This does not imply 'illusory', but rather 'diabolic'. Both kinds of magic, natural and 'black', were believed in in the Middle Ages, though only natural magic was approved of by the orthodox. There has so far been no definite indication that the Clerk is employing anything but natural magic; the Franklin is evidently determined to be on the side of respectable orthodoxy.

601. *tables Tolletanes* Astronomical tables were necessary for the practice of astrology, and the most widely used ones (on which Chaucer based his own *Equatorie of the Planetis*) were the Alfonsine tables, drawn up for the longitude of Toledo in Spain (hence *Tolletanes*) in the thirteenth century.

602. *corrected* Tables based on the longitude of Toledo would have to be modified for use in Brittany.

603-4. The *root* of a set of tables is the first date for which figures are given. A table for *collect* years is one enabling calculations to be made for long periods of time, from twenty years upwards, while a table for *expans* years gives figures for shorter periods of time. The two together would enable a planet's positions in any given year to be calculated.

605. *as been* 'such as'. *centris* The centres of the various circles in which the planets move. *argumentz* The angles governing a planet's position in its epicycle.

606. *proporcioneles convenientz* Figures for calculating the positions of planets during fractions of a year.

607. *equacions* Corrections to take account of minor motions.

608-11. According to the cosmology derived by the Middle Ages from Aristotle, the physical universe was arranged in nine concentric spheres, with the earth at the centre, and the Primum Mobile, which gave motion to all the rest, at the outside. The 'fixed' stars (i.e. those which were not planets) were in the eighth sphere. The twelve houses of the zodiac were usually measured in the ninth sphere, and took their names from the constellations with which they had originally coincided. Thus Alnath, a star in the constellation of Aries (the Ram), would originally have coincided with the zodiacal house of Aries. But the eighth sphere was in slow rotation (a fact which explained the precession of the equinoxes), and so the two no longer coincided. The Clerk knew how far they had moved apart, and took account of this in his calculation.

613. *firste mansioun* The first mansion (see note on lines 457–9) of the moon, which was called Alnath.

616. Each house of the zodiac was divided into equal parts called *faces* and into unequal parts called *termes*, and each *face* and *terme* was assigned to a particular planet. *Whos* therefore might refer either to a sign of the zodiac or to a planet.

617–18. The Franklin does not tell us which *was* the appropriate mansion of the moon for the experiment; we are evidently to be impressed without understanding. The next few lines are much vaguer.

632. Venus here does not seem to be 'astrologized', but to refer to the goddess of love.

652–3. Here the parody theology of love is used: just as man obtains salvation not by right but through God's free grace, so Aurelius begs for Dorigen's love. But there is something sinister in his modesty; he is keeping to the letter of the theology of love, but his whole speech *is* claiming her love as something due to him according to her promise.

671–3. Previously Dorigen had thought of the rocks as a *monstre*, something unnatural; now she thinks of their removal as such. Despite her earlier speech, complaining about the ordering of the universe, it appears now that she does after all believe in a natural order, a *proces of nature*, against which this magical illusion is an offence.

683–6. Dorigen begins another formal *pleynt* with an arraignment of Fortune, comparable with her earlier arraignment of God and his providence. Fortune is an important figure in medieval thought, and one of the seminal works behind the medieval conception of her is Chaucer's favourite *De Consolatione* of Boethius. Book II of the *De Consolatione* develops an elaborate image of Fortune as the force in control of all worldly events, dealing out prosperity and misery quite arbitrarily, and not according to men's deserts. She is visualized as a woman turning a great wheel, on which men rise and then fall. The chain that Dorigen here refers to is no doubt that by which men are attached to the wheel.

695–784. For comment on this list of twenty-two *exempla*, see Introduction, pp. 21–2 and 45–6.

696. At the end of the Peloponnesian War, the Thirty Tyrants seized power in Athens, murdering Phidon and instituting a tyranny.

707. 'The men of Messene had inquiries and searches made.'

711. *that she nas* 'who was not'.

715. Aristoclides was ruler of Orchomenos in Arcadia.

718. Diana was goddess of chastity. See note on line 373.

727-8. Hasdrubal was king of Carthage, the great rival city to Rome, when it was sacked by the Romans in the third Punic war.

730. *skipte* Judgements of the tone of words in fourteenth-century English are bound to be uncertain, but this word sounds light-hearted, in a way which undercuts the seriousness of the speech.

733-6. The story of Lucretia has become better known than most of the other *exempla*, partly no doubt through the influence of Shakespeare's poem *The Rape of Lucrece*. She was raped by Tarquin, and then committed suicide so as not to bring dishonour to her husband. Is it significant that Dorigen has now introduced an *exemplum* of a woman who killed herself *after* being raped, rather than before? Does it mean that this possibility has entered her own mind, or simply that she is becoming confused by her distress?

737-9. Miletus was sacked by the Gauls in the third century B.C.

742-6. Abradates was king of the Susi.

746. *if I may* 'if I can help it'.

754-5. Demotion's daughter killed herself when her fiancé died, so as not to be forced to marry someone else.

756-8. The daughters of Scedasus killed each other after being raped.

759-61. Nichanor was an officer of Alexander's at the capture of Thebes.

763. *for oon of Macidonye* 'because a man from Macedonia'.

765-6. The wife of Niceratus killed herself after her husband had been put to death by the Thirty Tyrants of Athens, so as to avoid falling into their hands herself. The case is remote from Dorigen's, though her vague *for swich cas* does something to conceal the fact.

767-9. Timandra, Alcibiades's mistress, insisted on burying his body after he had been murdered by the Thirty Tyrants.

768. *rather for to dien chees* 'chose rather to die'.

770. Alcestis died in place of her husband, Admetus.

771-2. Penelope was the wife of Odysseus; during his long absence, as recounted in the *Odyssey* of Homer, she was much pestered by suitors who took him to be dead, but she resisted them and he eventually returned.

773–5. When Protesilaus was killed by Hector at Troy, his wife Laodamia voluntarily accompanied him to the under-world.

776–8. Portia killed herself through anxiety about her husband Brutus.

779–80. Artemisia built a great sepulchre, or mausoleum, for her dead husband Mausolus. It is difficult to see what Dorigen could learn from the story.

781–2. Despite the double emphasis of *wyfly...wives*, it appears that Teuta was not married. Dorigen's *exempla* are becoming more and more desperately irrelevant. The idea of taking an event as a *mirour* (Latin *speculum*) or pattern for one's own life is a common one in medieval literature, which rarely fails to draw an explicit moral from a story.

783–4. Bilia showed her *parfit wyfhod* by putting up with her husband's bad breath; Rhodogune killed her nurse for trying to persuade her to marry a second time; Valeria refused to marry a second time.

793–4. As is natural in a poet writing for an audience of listeners, Chaucer manipulates his subject-matter explicitly, and, instead of simply not repeating himself, tells us that he is not going to repeat himself.

797. His reaction is startlingly mild—the very opposite of what we should expect. Dorigen's reply indicates her surprise.

798. *God helpe me so as wys!* Literally 'so indeed may God help me!'.

799. *and* 'if'.

800. Compare the proverb 'Let sleeping dogs lie'. Arveragus evidently sees Dorigen's agitated comment as the prelude to a recapitulation of the whole story, her feelings of guilt, etc., and wishes to avoid all this.

801. *paraventure* Pronounced (and sometimes spelt) 'paraunter'. This line is no doubt intended as a warning to *us* that the ending is not necessarily going to be tragic or even shameful, a warning amplified by the Franklin himself in lines 821–6. But there can be no guessing what in particular Arveragus is referring to in it—presumably it is intended merely as vague reassurance.

803. 'For as surely as I hope God will have mercy on me.'

807. *thing* This word seems to have here something of its older meaning of 'contract'.

808. His hitherto repressed emotion at last breaks out. But we shall perhaps be surprised to find that it is the thought of his reputation that produces his tears: he is concerned not with what is going to happen to his wife, but with what people will think of him. The reaction is in keeping with his initial stipulation that he must have *the name of soverainetee* in marriage, and with the Franklin's own concern with social status.

814. 'So that people can suspect or guess any evil of you.'

821-6. A brief digression, in which the Franklin directly addresses his listeners—a common feature of poetry intended for oral delivery.

833. 'And he was also on his way to the garden.' Verbs of motion can sometimes be omitted in Middle English.

837. *with glad entente* 'in happy expectation'.

840. Thus she openly admits her husband's *maistrie*, though paradoxically it has been exercised to give her up to another man.

851-2. The *cherlissh* is the exact opposite of the *gentil*. *Cherlissh* behaviour is what you would expect of a *cherl*, a lower-class person, while *gentillesse* is the ideal behaviour of an aristocrat. *Franchise* has approximately the same meaning as *gentillesse*, except that it implies more specifically generosity of behaviour.

854-60. In this extremely complicated sentence, 'and eek I se wel youre distresse' seems likely to be a parenthesis, with the sense carrying straight on from *gentillesse to yow* to *that him were levere*.

857. *him were levere han shame* 'he would rather be (publicly) humiliated'.

861-2. 'My lady, I return into your hands, as if discharged, every oath and every agreement.' Aurelius here and in the next two lines uses the legal language of a medieval release or quitclaim—language which is appropriate to the Franklin, with his legal experience (see *The General Prologue*, lines 355-6).

869-72. It is not clear (since quotation marks were not used in medieval manuscripts) whether these words are part of Aurelius's speech or whether they form a comment on the situation by the Franklin. In the light of the similarity in phrasing between lines 871-2 and the Clerk's boast in lines

939–40 (which are unquestionably spoken by the Clerk himself), it seems most likely that these lines too are spoken by the person to whom they refer.

869. 'But let every wife be careful what she promises!'

890. 'For all I can see, I am ruined.'

894. 'Unless I can obtain more mercy from him.'

897. *curteisye* Another of the key medieval ethical concepts is here introduced, along with *gentillesse*, *franchise*, and *trouthe*.

899. In the Middle Ages, it was normal for personal wealth to be stored in material form (such as gold, as here) in an iron-bound chest.

903. 'And allow him time to pay the balance.'

905. 'So far I have never failed to keep my word.'

908. 'Even if I go begging in my bare tunic.'

909. Having granted Dorigen a formal quitclaim, Aurelius is now trying to come to another legal arrangement with the Clerk.

921–2. Compare lines 793–4. This is clearly a formula of abbreviation, which the audience will understand as such, rather than a sign of poverty of language. The idiom of poetry intended to be read aloud will necessarily contain a large formulaic element, especially among the machinery of story-manipulation.

925. *were of hir trouthe fals* 'failed to keep her word'.

932–3. *Fre* (see line 950) and *frely* are the adjective and adverb corresponding to the noun *franchise* (see line 852 and note).

938–9. 'But God in his blessed power forbid that a scholar should not be able to perform a noble deed.'

942. Literally, 'as if you had crept out of the ground this very minute'—that is, as if you had just been born. Again a legal quitclaim is granted, though in somewhat fanciful language.

949–52. It was common for medieval poems of a courtly kind to end with an explicit question; Chaucer brings Part 1 of *The Knight's Tale* to an end in the same way. Here the purpose of the convention is particularly clear: where poetry is a form of communal entertainment, a pastime, it will fulfil its function most satisfactorily when it provides matter for discussion among the listeners when a particular poem is at an end. In this case we do not hear any discussion of the poem among the other pilgrims, such as we find elsewhere in *The Canterbury Tales*, because *The Franklin's Tale* is at the end of one of the manuscript fragments, and is not linked with any succeeding material.

APPENDIX

THE PORTRAIT OF THE FRANKLIN IN 'THE GENERAL PROLOGUE'

lines 333–62

A FRANKELEYN was in his compaignye.
Whit was his berd as is the dayesye;
Of his complexioun he was sangwin.
Wel loved he by the morwe a sop in wyn;
To liven in delit was evere his wone,
For he was Epicurus owene sone,
That heeld opinioun that pleyn delit
Was verray felicitee parfit.
An housholdere, and that a greet, was he;
Seint Julian he was in his contree.
His breed, his ale, was alweys after oon;
A bettre envined man was nowher noon.
Withoute bake mete was nevere his hous
Of fissh and flessh, and that so plentevous,
It snewed in his hous of mete and drinke,
Of alle deyntees that men koude thinke.
After the sondry sesons of the yeer,
So chaunged he his mete and his soper.
Ful many a fat partrich hadde he in muwe,
And many a breem and many a luce in stuwe.
Wo was his cook but if his sauce were
Poynaunt and sharp, and redy al his geere.
His table dormant in his halle alway
Stood redy covered al the longe day.
At sessiouns ther was he lord and sire;

Ful ofte time he was knight of the shire.
An anlaas and a gipser al of silk
Heeng at his girdel, whit as morne milk.
A shirreve hadde he been, and a contour.
Was nowher swich a worthy vavasour.

complexioun temperament   *morwe* morning
To liven...felicitee parfit see pages 3–4
Seint Julian see page 3   *after oon* up to the same standard
envined stocked with wine   *mete* food
snewed snowed, proliferated   *muwe* coop
luce pike   *stuwe* fish-pond   *poynaunt* pungent
table dormant fixed table
At sessiouns...sire he presided over the justices of the peace
knight of the shire member of parliament for his county
anlaas dagger   *gipser* purse   *shirreve* sheriff
contour auditor   *vavasour* landholder.

GLOSSARY

abegged begging

abide (inf. *abiden*) wait, stay, abstain

above (l. 483) in addition

accord agreement

acordaunt appropriate

acordeth (inf. *acorden*) agrees

adoun down

after after, afterwards; according to

again(s) against; back

ageyn back

al all; (followed by subjunctive verb) although; (l. 206) *al be they* although they are; (l. 455) *al were he* although he was; (l. 658) *al be that I* although I

Alcebiades Alcibiades

Alceste Alcestis

aleyes garden paths

allow (inf. *allowen*) praise

Alnath a star in Aries

als also

alwey constantly

amidde in the middle of

amonges among

amor(o)us in love

and and; (l. 799) if

ano(o)n at once; *anon-right* immediately

anoyeth (inf. *anoyen*) does harm

apaid (inf. *apayen*) pleased

apparence(s) illusion(s)

Appollo Apollo

arace (inf. *aracen*) tear away

argumentz see note on l. 605

aright correctly

arising rising

Armorik Armorica (a name for Brittany)

array dress

arrayed (inf. *arrayen*) adorned, arranged

artes sciences

Arthemisie Artemisia

artow (inf. *been*) art thou

arwe(s) arrow(s)

as as (if). Often redundant, especially in relative constructions

assaye (inf. *assayen*) attempt

asterte (inf. *asterten*) escape

astoned dumbfounded

aswage (inf. *aswagen*) diminish

atte at the

atteyne (inf. *atteynen*) overcome

Atthenes Athens

avantage (l. 100) *at his avantage* in a position of superiority

avaunt boast

aventure fortune; event

aventures happenings

aviseth (inf. *avisen*) *aviseth yow* consider

awaiteth (*on*) (inf. *awaiten*) watches (for)

ay always

baar (inf. *beren*) carried

bad (inf. *bidden*) ordered

Barbarie barbarian lands
bare (l. 48) unadorned
barge vessel
be (inf. *been*) been
been are, be
beest animal
berd beard
beren bear
beste best; (l. 545) *as for the beste* as the best thing to do
bet better
biforn before, in front of
bigon(ne) (inf. *biginnen*) began; (l. 644) *me is wo bigon* I am troubled by misery
bihe(e)ste promise
bihight(e)(n) (inf. *biheten*) promised
biholde (inf. *biholden*) look
bihoveth it is necessary (with dative pronoun)
bileve creed
Bilyea Bilia
birafte (inf. *bireven*) deprived
bisheche(th) (inf. *bisechen*) beseech(es)
biside by his side; (l. 230) *ther biside* near there
bisily diligently
bisinesse care, diligence
bitide (inf. *bitiden*) happen
bittre bitter, cruel
bitwix(e) between
biwreye (inf. *biwreyen*) reveal
blake black
blede (inf. *bleden*) bleed
blisful joyful; (l. 373) blessed
blisse happiness
bond agreement
boot boat
borwe (l. 562) *to borwe* as a pledge

bown prepared
brast (inf. *bresten*) burst out
brawen flesh
breste (inf. *bresten*) break
bresting breaking
breyde (inf. *breyden*) (l. 355) *out of his wit he breyde* he went out of his mind
brid bird
bringeth (inf. *bringen*) (l. 817) conduct
Britai(g)ne, Briteyne Brittany; Britain
Briton Breton
Britouns Bretons
bugle horn drinking horn
burel plain
burned burnished
but but; merely; (followed by subjunctive verb) unless; *but if* unless, except
cam (inf. *comen*) came
Cartage Carthage
cas matter, situation, reason
caught(e) (inf. *cacchen*) (l. 68) taken; (l. 848) conceived
cause (l. 44) *by cause* because
causelees without cause
Cedasus Scedasus
centris centres
certein, certeyn (adj.) (l. 194) sure; (l. 896) *at certeyn dayes* on fixed days
certein, certeyn (adv.) certainly
certes indeed
chalange (inf. *chalangen*) claim
chaunce fortune
chauninge change
cheere countenance, behaviour; (l. 426) *maketh hire good cheere* entertains her
chees (inf. *chesen*) chose

cherisseth (inf. *cherissen*) cherishes

cherlissh ignoble, ungracious

chese (inf. *chesen*) choose

cheyne chain

chiere countenance, expression; (l. 585) *dooth...chiere and reverence* behaves pleasantly and respectfully

chiertee love

chivalrie knighthood

clene free

cleped (inf. *clepen*) called

clerk(es) scholar(s) (see Appendix to *An Introduction to Chaucer*)

cofre chest

colde (adj.) gloomy

colde (inf. *colden*) (l. 351) grow cold

collect see note on ll. 603-4

colours see Introduction, p. 19

comen (inf. *comen*) come, descended

compaignye company; (l. 91) *holden compaignye* keep company

complaine (inf. *complainen*) lament

compleint(es) laments

complexioun disposition (see note on l. 110)

compleyning lament

comth (inf. *comen*) comes, arrives

comune (inf. *comunen*) converse

conclusio(u)n (l. 217) summing up; (l. 342) result of discussion; (l. 591) experiment

confort (l. 154) consolation; (l. 495) encouragement

conforten (inf. *conforten*) comfort

considered (inf. *consideren*) observable

constellacioun see note on l. 109

constreyned (inf. *constreynen*) forced, compelled

contenance expression

contrarien oppose

contree country

coome (inf. *comen*) came

coost coast

coppe cup

corrected adapted, modified

cost expenditure

cours course

craft skill, art

crie (inf. *cryen*) (l. 824) *upon her crie* condemn her

cropen (inf. *crepen*) crept

curious occult, esoteric

curiously elaborately

cursednesse wickedness

curteisye courtesy (see Appendix to *An Introduction to Chaucer*)

dauncen (inf. *dauncen*) dance

dawes days

day(es) day(s); *day ne night* at any time; (l. 903) *dayes of* time to pay

declinacion altitude

dede dead

dedly dying

dees dice

defaute fault

defoulen defile

degree status

delit pleasure

delitables delightful

Delphos Delphi

demen (l. 814) *demen harm*
suspect evil

demeth (inf. *demen*) judge

Demociones Demotion's

departe (inf. *departen*) part,
split

derke dark, gloomy

descended (inf. *descenden*) (l.
570) *been descended* got down

desdeyn (l. 28) *haveth...in
desdeyn* be offended with

despende (inf. *despenden*) waste

despeyred, despeired in despair

despit (l. 699) cruelty; (l. 723)
contempt

destreyneth (inf. *destreynen*)
torments

dette debt

devise (inf. *devisen*) describe

deyde (inf. *dyen*) died

deye (inf. *dyen*) die

deyntee (*of*) pleasure (in)

Dianes Diana's

diligence (l. 586) utmost

dirke dark

disconfort distress

discrecioun discernment

discrive (inf. *discriven*)
describe

disese sorrow

dispeyred in despair

disport recreation

disporte (inf. *disporten*) amuse

disputison disputation

diverse various

do (inf. *doon*) cause (to), make;
(l. 306) *do me deye* cause me
to die; (l. 384) *do...do* perform...make

doghtres daughters

doom (ll. 5, 256) *as to my doom*
by my judgement

doon do, perform, commit

dooth (inf. *doon*) do(es)

dorste (inf. *durren*) dared,
durst

doute fear

drede (noun) fear; *withouten
drede, it is no drede* without
doubt

drede (inf. *dreden*) fear,
reverence

dredful fearful

dreynte (inf. *drenchen*)
drowned

drive (inf. *driven*) (l. 558)
completed

drough (inf. *drawen*) drew,
approached

duren remain

ech each

eek also

eft again

eighe eye

eighte eighth

eke also

Ekko Echo

elles, ellis else

emperisse empress

emprented (inf. *emprenten*)
imprinted

emprenting impression

emprise undertaking

endelong all along

endite (inf. *enditen*) write

endure(n) last

Engelond England

enquere (inf. *enqueren*) in-
quire

ensamples examples, *exempla*

entende (inf. *entenden*) (l. 17)
apply himself

entendeth (inf. *entenden*) pays
attention

entente (ll. 287, 310) meaning; (ll. 506, 820) plan; (l. 711) will; (l. 837) expectation

equacions see note on l. 607

er(st) before

ese ease, comfort

eterne eternal

evene uniformly

everich every, each

evericho(o)n everyone

everydeel every bit

expans see note on ll. 603–4

eyen eyes

fader father

fadme fathoms

fadres (l. 701) father's

fantasye fantasies, imaginings

fare (inf. *faren*) gone; (l. 907) get on; *fare amis* be unlucky

faringe (l. 260) *beste faringe* handsomest

faste close

fasteth (inf. *fasten*) does not eat

fauconers falconers

feeleth (inf. *feelen*) (l. 55) *feeleth noght of* is unaffected by

feelingly with feeling

feendly fiendish

feere fear

feestes feasts

feith faith

felawe companion

fer(ther) far(ther)

feste feast

figure image

fil(le) (inf. *fallen*) fell; (l. 69) *fil of his accord* came to an agreement with him; (l. 292) *fille in speche* struck up conversation; (l. 445) *him fil in*

remembraunce it came into his memory; (l. 547) *fille they in tretee* they began negotiating

fir fire

firste (l. 3) original

fixe fixed

flood flood-tide

flour(es) flower(s)

folwen follow

folweth (inf. *folwen*) follows

for for; because; (l. 72) *for to* so as to

forbede (inf. *forbeden*) forbid

fordo (inf. *fordoon*) ruined

forlorn (inf. *forlesen*) completely lost

forme appearance

forth forward, out; (l. 292) continually; (l. 831) *forth right* direct

forthward forward

foul ugly

franchise generosity

Fraunce France

freendes friends; (l. 90) lovers

fre(ly) generous(ly)

fresshe bold; bright

fressher livelier

fro from

ful very

furius raging

fy fie

Galathee Galatea

gan (inf. *ginnen*) began (often used as an auxiliary verb to indicate the past tense)

Gawle Gaul

geeris equipment

gentil noble (see Introduction, pp. 8–9, and Appendix to *An Introduction to Chaucer*) *gentillesse* noble behaviour, magnanimity (see Introduction, pp. 8–9, and Appendix to *An Introduction to Chaucer*)

gentilly nobly (see Introduction, pp. 8–9, and Appendix to *An Introduction to Chaucer*)

gerdon reward

Gerounde Gironde

gesse (inf. *gessen*) suppose

gilt fault, guilt

giltelees guiltless

glade (inf. *gladen*) cheer

glide (inf. *gliden*) flow

go (inf. *goon*) go, walk

gon (inf. *goon*) gone

gonne (inf. *ginnen*) began

go(o)n go, pass, walk; (l. 553) act; (l. 105) *so moot I goon* I assure you

goon (inf. *goon*) (ll. 349, 679) gone

go(o)th (inf. *goon*) go(es)

governaunce (l. 114) self-control; (l. 194) control

grace mercy, favour; (l. 894) *bettre grace* more mercy

graunte (inf. *graunten*) consent, allow

grave (inf. *graven*) buried

graven engrave

greet, grete great

grette (inf. *greten*) greeted

gretteste greatest

grevaunce distress

greve (inf. *greven*) harm

grisly horrible

Habradate Abradates

halke nook

han (inf. *ha(ve)n*) have

happe(d) (inf. *happen*) chance(d), occur(red)

Hasdrubales Hasdrubal's

hastily quickly

hastow (inf. *ha(ve)n*) hast thou

haukes hawks

heed head

heele prosperity

heep lot

heerbiforn before this

heere (adv.) here

heere (inf. *heeren*) hear

heerof of this

heet (inf. *hoten*) called

heigh high; (ll. 63, 101) noble; (l. 177) *an heigh* above; (l. 851) great

hem them

hemself, hemselven themselves

hente (inf. *henten*) seized

herberwe position

herd(e) (inf. *heren*) heard

here (l. 118) her

heritage inheritance

herkneth (inf. *herknen*) listen to

herne cranny

heste promise

hethen heathen

hevinesse grief

hevy gloomy

hewe colour, brightness

hewed coloured

hight (inf. *hoten*) promise(d); (l. 852) made her promise

hir(e) her; their

hirselven herself

his his, its

holde (inf. *holden*) held

holden (inf. *holden*) held; keep; (l. 822) consider

holdeth (inf. *holden*) keep

holpen (inf. *helpen*) helped

hom home
hond hand
hool whole, wholly; (l. 439) unwounded
hooly holy
hoom home
hoote hot
housbonde husband
humblesse humility
hye(ste) high(est)
idel vain
illusioun (l. 592) deception
imaginatif suspicious
inpossible (adj.) impossible
inpossible (noun) impossibility
ire anger
jalousie jealousy
japes tricks
jogelrye conjuring
jolier gayer
jupartie danger
justeth (inf. *justen*) jousts
justing jousting
kalkuled (inf. *kalkulen*) calculated
kan (inf. *konnen*) can, am able, know; (l. 43) *as I kan*, (l. 326) *in al that evere I kan* as best I can; (l. 114) *kan on* is capable of; (l. 584) *in al that evere he kan* in every possible way; (l. 590) *that he kan* as much as possible
kene sharp
kepe (inf. *kepen*) keep, preserve
kinde nature (see Appendix to *An Introduction to Chaucer*)
kinrede kindred, family
kirtle tunic
kithe (inf. *kithen*) show
knit (inf. *knitten*) (l. 314)

bound by marriage; (l. 558) agreed
knowe (inf. *knowen*) known
knowes (noun) knees
koude (inf. *konnen*) could
Lacedomye Lacedaemonia, Sparta
lakked (inf. *lakken*) there was lacking (with dative pronoun); (l. 514) *hem lakked* they lacked
langour sickness
langwissheth (inf. *langwisshen*) endures pain
Laodomya Laodamia
large free
lasse less
lat (inf. *leten*) let
laton copper
layes (l. 275) songs
lede(n) (inf. *leden*) lead
ledest (inf. *leden*) governest
leeste least; *at the leeste wey* at least; (l. 870) *atte leeste* at the very least
leet(e) (inf. *leten*) allowed; (l. 707) *leete enquere and seke* had inquiries and searches made
leeve dear
leiser opportunity
lenger longer; (l. 790) *ever lenger the moore* continually more and more
leo(u)n lion; (l. 386) Leo, a sign of the zodiac (see note on ll. 385–6)
lerneth (inf. *lernen*) learn
lese (inf. *lesen*) lose
leste (adj.) least
lest(e) (verb) see *list(e)*
lete (inf. *leten*) leave, let

117

lette (inf. *letten*) hinder

leve (inf. *leven*) leave off, give up

levere rather; (l. 20) *hath levere* prefers; (l. 688) *have I levere* I prefer; (ll. 850, 857) *him were levere* he would prefer; (l. 859) *I have wel levere* I would greatly prefer

leves (noun) leaves

lewed ignorant, stupid .

lighte (inf. *lighten*) descended; (l. 511) *doun of...lighte* got down from

liketh (inf. *liken*) it pleases; (l. 146) *whan hem liketh* when it pleases them, when they please

lisse relief

lissed (inf. *lissen*) relieved

list(e), *lest(e)* (no inf.) (usually with dative pronoun) desire, wish, like

listeth (no inf.) (usually with dative pronoun) desires, wishes, likes

lith (inf. *lyen*) lies; (l. 665) *in yow lith al* it lies entirely in your power

live (l. 260) *on live* alive

lond land

longen belong

looke(th) look; see (to it); (l. 320) *looke what day* whatever day

looth hateful (with dative pronoun); (l. 847) *looth him was* he was unwilling

lordshipe mastery, dominion

lorn (inf. *lesen*) lost

lothest most unwilling

Lucresse Lucretia

lust pleasure, desire

lusty (l. 265) pleasant; (l. 583) jovial

lyf life

lyk like

lykerous eager

lym lime, mortar

maad (inf. *maken*) made

Macidonye Macedonia

maden (inf. *maken*) (they) made

maidenhede virginity

maister expert

maistres (l. 548) expert's

maistrie, maistrye domination

make (inf. *maken*) make, create, cause, perform

maner(e) manner, way, kind (of)

mansioun(s) station(s) (see note on ll. 457–9)

mate(e)re matter(s); (l. 275) theme

may (no inf.) may, can; (l. 746) *if I may* if I can help it

Mecene Messene

mede meadow

meenes instruments

meke humble

men people; one

mente (inf. *menen*) meant

merciable merciful

merk image

merveille marvel

merveillous marvellous

meschaunce misfortune

meschaunces cursed acts

Milesie Miletus

mirour mirror, example

mo more

monstre unnatural thing

moone complaint

moorneth (inf. *moornen*)
mourns, yearns

moot(e) (no inf.) must

morwe morning; (l. 229)
morwe-tide time of morning

moste must

muchel much

myn my, mine

myselven myself

name name, reputation

namely especially

namoore no more

Narcisus Narcissus

nas (inf. *been*) was not

nat not

nathelees nevertheless

naturelly by its nature

ne not, nor

necligence negligence

nedes necessarily

nedeth (inf. *neden*) (it) is
necessary

Neptunus Neptune

nere (inf. *been*) were not

Nicerates Niceratus's

Nichanore Nichanor

nis (inf. *been*) is not

noght nothing; not at all; (l.
149) *sette at noght* valued at
nothing

nolde (inf. *willen*) would not

noon none; nobody; not

nought nothing

Nowel see note on l. 583

ny nearly

o one

obeisaunce submissiveness

observaunces customary rites

ofte often

oght anything

oghte (inf. *owen*) ought

Omer Homer

oold former

oon one

operacioun (l. 618) experiment

operaciouns (l. 457) working

opposicion see note on ll. 385–6

oppressed (inf. *oppressen*)
violated

ordinaunce arrangements

orisonte horizon

orisoun prayer

Orliens Orleans

oute away

outher either

overspringe (inf. *overspringen*)
rise above

owene own

pacient long-suffering

page servant

paine (l. 58) *dide his paine*
took trouble

paraventure perhaps

parcel part

pardee indeed (a common mild
oath)

parfit perfect

particuler out of the way

passinge surpassing

Pedmark Penmarc'h

peere equal

Penalopee Penelope

penaunce suffering

Pernaso Parnassus

peyne pain, sorrow; (ll. 184,
302) *peynes smerte* pain of
sorrow; (l. 809) *up peyne of*
on pain of

peynte(d) (inf. *peynten*)
paint(ed)

Phebus Phoebus (Apollo)

philosophre scientist

pitee pity, compassion

pitous sorrowful

pitously pitiably

plain field of contest

plesaunce pleasure, delight

pley (noun) jest

pleye(n) play; amuse (themselves); (l. 469) perform

pleyn plain

pleyne (on) (inf. *pleynen*) complain (against)

pleyneth (inf. *pleynen*) laments

pleynt lamentation

plighte(n) (inf. *plighten*) pledge(d)

Porcia Portia

possibilitee (l. 671) *by possibilitee* by any possibility

prechen (inf. *prechen*) exhort

preieth (inf. *preyen*) pray

preise (inf. *preisen*) commend

preyde (inf. *preyen*) begged

preyeth (inf. *preyen*) begs

prively secretly; (l. 69) in private; (l. 456) covered up

proces process; (l. 157) *by proces* gradually

profre propose (for)

proporcioneles convenientz see note on l. 606

proporcioun adjustment

Protheselaus Protesilaus

prys excellence; (l. 262) esteem

pured (inf. *puren*) refined

purposinge intending

purveiaunce providence; (l. 232) provisions

queynte strange

quik alive

quiked (inf. *quiken*) kindled

quikkest busiest

quit (ll. 691, 862) discharged

quod (inf. *quethen*) said

rage madness (of sorrow)

raving delirium

redden (inf. *reden*) read

reden (l. 448) study

redressed (inf. *redressen*) avenged

reft (inf. *reven*) robbed of

regioun realm

reherce (inf. *rehercen*) repeat

reine rule

rele(e)sse (inf. *relessen*) remit, return; (l. 941) set free

remembraunce memory

remembre (inf. *remembren*) remind

remenaunt remainder

remoeved (inf. *remoeven*) moved

remoeve(n) remove

repreve (of) (inf. *repreven*) reproach (about)

resoun reason

respiten grant respite

rethorik rhetoric

revel revelry

reverence respect

reweth (inf. *rewen*) have pity

reyn rain

right (adv.) just, exactly, directly; (l. 12) *right now* at this very moment

righte (adj.) direct; true

rigour severity

rimeyed written in rhyming verse

river (l. 524) hawking ground

Rodogone Rhodogune

rokkes rocks

Romayn(s) (the) Roman(s)

romen (l. 171) *romen hire* wander about

rominge wandering
rootes see note on ll. 603–4
roundels see note on l. 276
routhe (a) pity
rude rough
said (inf. *seyn*) (l. 875) say
Saine Seine
salewed (inf. *salewen*) greeted
saleweth (inf. *salewen*) greets
saufly safely
saugh (inf. *seen*) saw
save (preposition) except (for)
save (inf. *saven*) maintain
say (inf. *seen*) saw
sayn see *seyn*
Scithero Cicero
se (inf. *seen*) see
secree secretly
see sea
seen see
seeth (inf. *seen*) sees
seide (inf. *seyn*) said
seigh (inf. *seen*) saw
seillinge sailing
seith (inf. *seyn*) says
seke(n) search
selve same, very
semed (inf. *semen*) (it) seemed
(with dative pronoun); ap-
peared
semen (inf. *semen*) seem
sene see; (l. 439) *withoute for
to sene* to look at from outside
serement oath
servage subjection
service devotion
seten (inf. *sitten*) sat
seuretee security
sey(e)(n) (inf. *seyn*) say
seyde (inf. *seyn*) said
seyn (inf. *seen*) (l. 520) seen

seyn, sayn say, tell, repeat
seyth (inf. *seyn*) say
shame (noun) shame, humiliation; *for shame of* out of
regard for
shame(n) (verb) put to shame
sheene bright
sholde (inf. *shullen*) should
shoon (inf. *shinen*) shone
shoop (inf. *shapen*) (l. 137)
shoop him arranged,
planned
shopen (inf. *shapen*) arranged
shortly briefly
shoures showers
shove (inf. *shoven*) moved
forward
shul (inf. *shullen*) shall; must
sike sick
siker(ly) certain(ly)
sikes sighs
siketh (inf. *siken*) sighs
sin since
sires (ladies and) gentlemen
sit (inf. *sitten*) sits
sith since
sixte sixth
skipte (inf. *skippen*) leapt
slake (inf. *slaken*) abate
sle(e)(n) kill
sleep (inf. *slepen*) (have) slept
sleeth (inf. *sleen*) kills
slide (inf. *sliden*) slip away
slitte (inf. *slitten*) pierce
slouthe laziness
slow(e) (inf. *sleen*) killed
smerte pain
snybbed (inf. *snybben*) scolded
so so, such; *so that* if
sobrely gravely
socour aid
sodeyn(ly) immediate(ly)

Glossary

softe gentle
solas comfort, pleasure, delight
somme (noun) sum
somme (pronoun) some
songe (inf. *singen*) sang
sonken (inf. *sinken*) sunk
sonne sun
soor (l. 899) heavy
soore deeply, bitterly
sooth (the) truth
sope(e)r supper
sorwe(ful) sorrow(ful)
sothe truth
soupe (inf. *soupen*) have supper
soverainetee supremacy
soverein supreme
spak (inf. *speken*) spoke, said
spedde (inf. *speden*) (l. 590)
  spedde him hastened
speere sphere
squier squire
stable immutable
stant (inf. *standen*) stands
stirt(e) (inf. *stirten*) sprang,
  leapt
stoon stone
straunge (l. 551) *made it*
  straunge held off
stryf quarrelling
Stymphalides Stymphalis
stynten cease (talking)
subtil(e) expert
subtilly expertly
suffise (inf. *suffisen*) be capable
suffraunce forbearance
suffre (inf. *suffren*) endure, be
  patient, permit
suffreth (inf. *suffren*) (l. 462)
  permits
supersticious diabolic
sursanure wound healed over
  on the surface

sustene (inf. *sustenen*) keep up
suster sister
swerd sword
swich(e) such
swoor (inf. *sweren*) swore
swowne swoon
swyn boar
taak (inf. *taken*) take
tables backgammon
take (inf. *taken*) taken
tarie (inf. *tarien*) delay
teeris tears
temperaunce moderation, self-
  restraint
thanne then
the(e) thee
thennes thence, from there
ther there, where
therby near it
therto moreover; of it
thider there, to it
thilke the same, that
thing thing; contract; *no thing*
  not at all
thinketh (inf. *thinken*) it seems
  (with dative pronoun)
this this (is)
thise the; these
tho then
thogh though
thoght thought, care,
  melancholy
thonketh (inf. *thonken*) thanks
thoughte (inf. *thinken*) it
  seemed (with dative
  pronoun)
thral slave
thridde third
thriftily politely
thritty thirty
thurgh through
thyn thy, thine

time time; (ll. 294, 591) opportunity; (l. 113) *after the time* according to the occasion

tiraunt(z) tyrants

to to; too

Tolletanes Toledan

tonge language

touchinge concerning

toun town, city

travaille labour

tregetour(e)s conjurers

trespas sin

tretee negotiation

trewe faithful

trewely truly

Troie Troy

trouthe (pledged) word; (l. 87) *have heer my trouthe* I hereby promise

turned (inf. *turnen*) (l. 339) *turned him* went away

tweyne two

under (l. 437) within

undertake (inf. *undertaken*) declare

unnethe(s) hardly

unresonable contrary to reason

untrewe unfaithful

unwiting (of) unknown (to)

usage habit

useden (inf. *usen*) practised

venquisseth (inf. *venquissen*) overcomes

verray, verrey real, very, true

vertu virtue; but see note on l. 8

vertuous accomplished

vileynye dishonour (see Appendix to *An Introduction to Chaucer*)

virelayes see note on l. 276

vitaille food

voided (inf. *voiden*) (they) dismissed

vouche(th) sauf (inf. *vouchen sauf*) grant, consent

waiten watch out for

waketh (inf. *waken*) stays awake

wan (inf. *winnen*) (had) conquered

war wary, careful

warisshed (inf. *warisshen*) cured

wax (inf. *wexen*) grew

weel well

weep (inf. *wepen*) wept

wel (a vague intensifier) well, highly, certainly, completely, very, much; (l. 64) *wel unnethes* hardly

welfare well-being

welles springs

wende (inf. *wenden*) travel

wende (inf. *wenen*) expected

wene (inf. *wenen*) imagine

were (inf. *been*) were, would be

werk work; (l. 434) trouble; (l. 313) *word ne werk* word or deed

werre hostility

whan when; *whan so that* whenever

what what; why; *what for* what with

wheither whether

wher whether; *wher so* whether

where where; *where as* where(ver)

which which, who(m), what (a)

whiderward where

whiles while

wight person

wighte (l. 888) *of wighte* by weight

wirking motion

wise way, manner

wisly certainly, surely

wiste (inf. *witen*) knew

wit(tes) intelligence, understanding; (l. 355) mind, wits

withal also

withoute from outside

wo misery; (l. 335) *wo was*, unhappy was; (l. 644) *me is wo bigon*, I am troubled by misery

wol(e) (inf. *willen*) will, wish to

wolde(n) (inf. *willen*) would, wished to

wonder wonderful

wondren (on) wonder (at)

woost (inf. *witen*) knowest

woot (inf. *witen*) know

worshipe (l. 139) glory; (l. 290) reputation

worthinesse excellence

worthy noble, excellent

wowke week

wrapped (inf. *wrappen*) entangled

wrecche wretched

wrecchednesse wretched work or deed

wreken (inf. *wreken*) avenged

wreye (inf. *wreyen*) disclose

wro(u)ght(e) (inf. *werchen*) did, performed, made, produced

wyf(ly) wife(ly)

wyfhod wifeliness

wyke week

wyn wine

wys (adj.) prudent, wise

wys (adv.) indeed; (l. 798) *God helpe me so as wys* God help me indeed

yaf (inf. *yeven*) gave

ye (disyllable = noun) eye

ye (monosyllable = pronoun) you

yeer(is) year(s)

yerd garden

yet still

yeve(st) (inf. *yeven*) give(st)

yfinde (inf. *(y)finden*) find

yfostred (inf. *fostren*) nourished, benefited

yfounde (inf. *finden*) found

yit yet

yive (inf. *yeven*) given

yknowe (inf. *yknowen*) recognize

yknowen (inf. *knowen*) known

ylaft (inf. *leven*) left

ynogh, ynow enough

yoore, of time yoore since old times

ypayed (inf. *payen*) paid

yquit (inf. *quiten*) (reflexive) acquitted yourself

ysene visible

yslain (inf. *sleen*) killed

ystiked (inf. *stiken*) stabbed

ysworn (inf. *sweren*) sworn

yvoided (inf. *voiden*) removed

ywis indeed, surely